A STUDENT'S GUIDE TO COURSEWORK WRITING

Mary Coles

Cartoons by Bill Petherick

Acknowledgements

My grateful thanks to all those students at the University who have read the earlier versions of this book and suggested amendments.

And to Joyce Burn who spent many a happy hour making alterations to the umpteen "final" versions of this text.

I am also grateful to the EOC for permission to use their statistical information.

First published 1995
Copyright © Mary Coles 1995
ISBN 1 85769 024 9

Published by   **University of Stirling**

Copies obtainable from   **The Division of Educational Policy & Development**
Airthrey Castle
University of Stirling
Stirling FK9 4LA

Printed by   **Ritchie of Edinburgh**
163 Bonnington Road, Edinburgh, EH6 5RE

CONTENTS

How to use this book

 It is divided into 8 sections.
Each section is complete in itself and you may well not need to read the whole book. Just read what you need help with.

Section 1   **Some general guidelines about**

- what processes are involved in academic coursework writing
- the time involved

Section 2   **A step by step guide to writing a coursework essay** - a starting point from which you can develop a method that best suits you

Section 3   **Writing a report - how this differs from essay-writing**

SECTION 1

INTRODUCTION

Time and Timing

The amount of time needed to write an essay will vary tremendously between people and essays. Some will take 40+ hours, others less. But early essays will take most people a long time - if you are doing them properly!
Don't despair. Things will improve.

As a guide you will need time

- to consider the question and all the issues involved

- to get or order the books you need

- to do the reading and take notes

- to discuss it with other students

- to let it all sink in so you can select only what is relevant

- to put an initial argument together

- to explore different approaches

- to rank your ideas in order of importance

- to refine your arguments

- to go back to the books and look for proofs of points you have made

- to write first, second .... final drafts

- to leave it long enough to have forgotten the details so you can revise it with new eyes

This may all take four weeks. If this seems a long time, try it!

The processes involved

Academic coursework essays are probably very different from anything you've done before but they are central to most Higher Education courses. They are, in fact, one of the most important parts of the learning process at this stage of education because they force you into doing those things which Higher Education is generally designed to enable you to do. The fact that coursework writing is also a method by which your tutors can decide how well you have grasped the subject is - for you - of almost secondary importance!

To write a good essay you need to

- focus on a specific problem
- identify the most important issues involved
- identify the most suitable approaches
- explore the facts
- identify the principles underlying the facts
- examine the existing theories developed to account for the facts
- evaluate the relative value of these theories
- examine their implications
- come to a considered, balanced and reasoned judgement
- relate this issue to a wider context

In this way you gain a thorough understanding of the subject and identify appropriate ways of dealing with it. You can then make informed and reasoned judgements.

Coursework writing will most frequently take the form of essays. However, dissertatious reports, oral presentations and discussion documents all involve the same initial processes. Only the length and the last stages of production are different.

 Exam essays are very different. They are designed for a different purpose, come at a different stage in the learning process, and involve different skills. They are important - but not what this guide is all about.

SECTION 2

A GUIDE TO WRITING THE ESSAY

How to use this Guide

Where to start and what order to do things in, are things people find difficult when they first begin to write academic essays. So this guide will take the form of step-by-step instructions on what to do and when to do it. The order in which you do things is important.

Some of the following suggestions may seem very odd but they are designed to prevent your falling into a number of well-known essay-writing traps

- losing sight of the line of argument
- getting bogged down in detail
- not going into enough detail, and writing skeletal essays
- only getting to the point half way through
- wandering off into the irrelevant

Everyone has different ways of solving the same problem. Some are more efficient and effective than others, but we all have to do it in the way that suits us. You will find the best way for you during the course of your studies. This guide is a **suggested starting point.**

What follows is one method of writing essays that works for most people.
But it is just that — one good method, not the only good method.

- You are unlikely to get it right first time. Ideally, therefore you should do a dummy run using these instructions. Realistically, for most students pressure of work and lack of time make people unwilling to do "exercises".

  So try this method out with your first essay. Or, if you didn't, and your essays are producing poorer marks than you expected, try it out with the next one and see if it makes any difference.

- Eventually you will **develop your own method**

  One thing that will help you do this is to reflect on what you do as you write the essay. Write these reflections down if necessary so you can remember what you did and when you did it. In this way you will consciously, and therefore quickly, develop the best way of writing essays **for you**.

! Before you start - a word of warning !

Essays are intended to be one person's attempt to come to grips with understanding a complex subject and to demonstrate this understanding in writing. (The original French word **essaie** means **try**). To do this the essay-writer needs to explain the issues raised by the question, examine them from a number of different angles or in a number of different ways, and then give a reasoned justification of his/her own view of the subject.

Obviously, if you are going to do this successfully, you cannot limit yourself to what you already know or believe. To examine all the angles you have not already thought of you need to get ideas from other people. And many of these ideas will inevitably come from books and journals - although there are many other places you can get them from. You will then need to use a lot of these ideas from books in your essays.

But on each occasion you need to remember that this is **your** essay. It is **your** attempt to come to some conclusions about the issue. You must, therefore, **before you begin writing it**, know what **your** line of argument is going to be. You will have to use the views of other writers on an issue as well as expressing your ideas. But you must know where your argument is going before you can do this. **Other people's ideas** then become part of **your** argument. They are only relevant in so far as they fit into **your** line of reasoning.

 A piece of writing that simply reproduces other people's ideas is not an essay. A piece of writing that appears to be your own argument but is actually made up of a muddled and ill-assorted selection of other people's ideas, joined together with a few words of your own, is worse.

Step 1: Choosing your question

Being given a choice of questions is not always the advantage it can seem at first. Choosing the right one can be the most important thing your do in the whole coursework-writing process. There are no absolute rules as to how to do it because a lot will depend on you - your interests, your strengths and your weaknesses. There are, however, some general guidelines you can follow.

● **Choose a question that you are interested in** - not just something you know a lot about. If you are interested in what you are writing about, you will almost always interest the reader.

● **Learn to recognise "easy" and "difficult" questions.**

Most sets of assignments include questions of widely differing levels of difficulty. Much of the secret of producing good coursework assignments lies in choosing a question of the right degree of difficulty **for you**.

● If you are in any doubt about your ability to write essays or reports choose a question that you completely understand and can cope with fairly confidently. Don't choose one that is too difficult just because you think it will impress the reader more. If you make a mess of it, it won't!

● If you know the subject well and are confident about your writing skills choose one that is more challenging. Don't go for the easy option if you can tackle something more difficult. You need to give yourself the opportunity to develop your thinking and writing skills - otherwise there is little point in doing all this study in the first place! There is no need to worry that by doing this you are automatically condemning yourself to a lower mark. Most markers take the difficulty of the question into account when they assess your writing.

- ## The easiest questions are those with the most clearly defined limits.

They often appear off-putting because they are long questions. The length is, in fact, a help because the person who wrote the question is giving you some idea of how to structure the answer in the way the question has been phrased.

Example

'At the root of the opposition to European economic, monetary and political integration in the two main political parties, is an out-dated attachment to the idea of the nation state'. How far do you consider this to be true?

This question defines the areas it wants you to cover very specifically. You are asked to deal with

- the **two main political parties** (not the rest)

- only **economic, monetary and political integration.**

- whether the attitude of the parties to these three things is the result of **an out-dated attachment to the idea of the nation state.**

The question has therefore suggested a structure for your essay - for the first part of it at least. You need to show how the attitude of the two parties to these three things is the result of an outdated attachment to the idea of the nation state.

The long instruction that follows the quotation also helps you by suggesting there may well be other reasons for their opposition as well and it would be relevant to discuss them.

Your conclusion is also suggested by the question. It needs to be your final judgement as to importance of the reason for the opposition mentioned in the question in relation to all the other reasons you've mentioned.

Hence the longer the question the more helpful it can be.

- ## The most apparently difficult questions are ones containing words you don't understand.

They can present problems but they are not usually the most insurmountable ones. Sometimes the word you don't understand is part of the quotation that precedes the actual question and it isn't fundamental to meaning anyway. Sometimes it is an essential part of the question but it is quite easy to find out its meaning.

In any case don't be put off the question **simply** because it contains a word you don't understand without looking it up. (The situation is obviously different in exams when you can't look things up). Equally important, though, don't attempt to do an essay without being **absolutely certain** of the meaning of all the words in the actual question. Be careful, too, with words you **think** you know the meaning of but are not very familiar with. You can easily misinterpret words in this way and go off on a disastrously wrong track.

- ## Some of the most difficult questions are those with no clearly defined limits.

This vagueness can take a number of different forms. Sometimes exactly what areas of the subject are being highlighted by the question are not clearly stated. And sometimes the words used are simply ambiguous.

Example 1

'The media do not shape public opinion so much as reflect it.'
Discuss.

Before you can start answering a question like this you have to decide on the limits. Which media are you going to deal with? Just those in Britain? What about the media in Britain that are actually part of an international network?

And what does the question mean by **public opinion**? Does it refer to consciously held opinions, or more deep-seated, unconscious ideology? And public opinion on what? On relatively superficial issues like who should succeed to the throne or whether British Summer Time should be retained? Or on more basic thing like politics, social policy and economics? Or even more fundamental things like race and gender?

Example 2

'Pressure groups exist to promote selfish interests; hence any steps taken to reduce their power will enhance the public interest' Discuss.

The answer to this question turns on your interpretation of **selfish interests** and **the public interest**. It could give you the opportunity to write a really thoughtful discussion of these terms, relating them to the subject of pressure groups.

However, if you are not exactly sure of what is meant by them or what the question is asking you to consider you could end up writing a purely descriptive essay on the workings of pressure groups or, alternatively, a long and rambling discussion of what the key terms mean.

You may also, without realising it, interpret the key terms in a peculiarly personal way which most people would find eccentric or unacceptable. This would invalidate your subsequent argument in the eyes of many readers.

This kind of question can therefore give you the opportunity for a really interesting discussion. But it can also give you the opportunity

- to misinterpret the questioner's intention,
- to choose inappropriate subject areas for discussion,
- to tackle it in very narrow or superficial way
- to try to cover far too many issues,
- to deal with a fairly random selection of ideas and to wander from point to point with very little sense of direction.

Therefore, choose the question you are going to answer according to your confidence, interest, knowledge and understanding.

Step 2: The vital first stage of planning

- **Read the question and think about it before you know too much about the topic!**

- **Write down your initial thoughts on how you think you might answer the question - a kind of preliminary plan.**

This will be no more than your initial, common-sense thoughts on the subject. Do it before you do much reading. If it is a completely new topic you may need to read one or two general discussions of it or go to a lecture or seminar on the subject. But it is essential to write this initial plan very early on in the process. You may not actually use it as the structure for your finished essay at all. But if you get bogged down in detail later on you can go back to it to see where you should be going.

Before you write this plan, however, you must have a clear idea of what the question is actually asking you to do.

Step 3: Understanding what you are being asked to do

● Look at the instruction words

These are the first important words to look at in any question. If you consider them carefully they will help you focus your answer and produce a balanced argument. The instruction words tell you what you have to do in your essay. Students often think they have been selected at random and mean much the same thing.
They haven't - and they don't!

Some Examples

The instruction words have been printed in bold.

- **Describe** the main stages involved in generating a corporate strategic plan.

- **Explain** how formal planning procedures could help any company you know well in determining future strategy.

- **Analyse** the role of the World Bank in the process of development in any one African country.

- Some critics allege Grierson's films reveal him to be profoundly conservative, even authoritarian. **Assess** the evidence for and against this judgement.

- "God is dead". **Discuss**

- **Consider** the influence of Ernest Hemingway on the work of Scott Fitzgerald.

- "The term 'the Hungry 30s' is a misleading description of living standards in that decade " **How far do you agree?**

- **Compare** the nature of urban development in Africa with that in Latin America.

Despite the notorious slipperiness of words in general, over the years a consensus has grown as to what the most common instruction words mean. In the following list words with similar meanings have been grouped together and their meaning explained. They are listed in ascending order of complexity. (There are no prizes for identifying which ones occur most frequently in University level essay titles!)

Major instruction words

Describe, Outline   means give a logical, accurate and detailed account of the main features of a subject

Summarise   means much the same - only briefly. Omit details.

Explain, Interpret, Account for   means describe the facts but also give causes and reasons for them. Depending on the context, these words may also suggest that you need to make the possible implications clear as well. **Explain X and its importance for Y** is an example.

Comment on, Criticise, Evaluate, Assess   all ask you to judge the value of something or the relative value of a number of things. Before you can do this you need to analyse, describe and explain each issue, theory or idea. Then you need to go through the arguments for and against each one. **At this stage no-one should be able to tell what your opinion is. All sides of the argument need to be laid out neutrally. Only in the section where you come to judgements should your views be clear.** It is very important that your judgements are also backed by reasons and evidence.

Discuss, Consider   are the least specific of the instruction words. You have to decide, first of all, what the main issues are. Then you follow the same procedure as for **Comment on, Criticise, Evaluate** and **Assess.**

How far, How true, To what extent   suggest there are various views on the subject. You need to outline some of them, evaluate their strengths and weaknesses, and then give your judgement. In fact all these instruction words suggest that there is more than one aspect to the subject, more than one judgement possible. You need to explore the alternatives.

! Beware *!*

- Even though they do not say so explicitly

  - **Explain** means **describe** and **explain**.
  - **Discuss** means **describe, explain** and **evaluate**.

- Even if they do not explicitly say so most of these instruction words involve dealing with an issue from a number of different angles, or discussing a number of possible theories or judgements. **Questions rarely imply you should put forward a passionate argument for one view only.**

- The main **exceptions** are when you are asked to **Justify** or **Refute**.

  - **Justify** means that you **explain, with evidence, why something is the case** (answering the main objections to your view as you go along).
  - **Refute** means you should **give evidence to prove why something is not the case.**

Instruction words involving comparison or contrast

Compare, Contrast, Distinguish, Differentiate, Relate all require that you discuss how things are related to each other.

Compare suggests you concentrate on similarities, **Contrast** on dissimilarities.

These words suggest that two situations/ideas/texts can be compared in a number of different ways, or from a variety of different angles. (Questions asking whether one view or another is correct and which begin **'Who........'** or **'Which.......'** require the same sort of treatment).

At first this looks simple. You just take each text/idea/situation in turn and do what you would do in a "normal" essay - analyse it to decide to on its key features, then describe, explain and discuss each one. When you have done them separately relate them to each other in the conclusion.

Example

Compare three different theories of Management Change

It is unlikely that the three theories will be exactly parallel. One may be a broad and generalised approach covering the causes of change, the problems it brings, and possible strategies for overcoming resistance. Another may deal specifically with the causes or strategies only. Under these circumstances it makes sense to break down your discussion by subject - causes, problems, strategies - and to discuss the various theories at the appropriate point in your overall argument. In this way the issues form the basis of your overall argument and you deal with the theories at the point at which they are relevant. Your conclusion would give your judgement on the relative value of each of the theories, with your reasons for that judgement.

Another example

Compare two novels by Graham Greene

One way of doing this is to

- Decide on the important features the novels have in common -themes, plot, characters, for example.
- Describe one novel first, concentrating on these features. Then do the same with the other. Finally, in a long conclusion deal with the points of comparison - characters, plot events, themes - one by one.

There is another way of doing it, however

- Select one important feature - characters, plot events, themes - as the subject of each section of your argument, and show how it is dealt with in each novel. Sum up their overall similarities/differences in the conclusion.

The first of these methods is the easiest. And when the **two things being compared are not clearly parallel** then it is often the best way. You will not then try to force the two into the same mould in order to fit the question. You can often miss the real point of both if you do this.

However, if you were asked to deal with something like two newspaper articles on the same events - that is, **two texts that are closely parallel** - then the second is probably more suitable because it will involve less repetition.

Secondary - but important instruction words

**Suggest,
Make Recommendations**

Some questions include two instruction words. These usually follow **Assess** or **Discuss** and mean that, in the light of your previous discussion, you should make proposals for changes or choices and defend why these are the proposals you have made. You also need to say why you think they would work or why they are better than the alternatives.

Illustrate

means you should back up your statements, judgements and ideas with evidence, often in the form of examples.

Even if the question doesn't ask you to illustrate - do it anyway!

(Of this, more later in Step 10!)

Interpreting the question appropriately is one of the more important steps in the whole essay-writing process. It's important to spend time, mental energy and a lot of discussion with other people on it.

Step 4 : Generating your essay plan from the wording of the question

● **Find and interpret the key issue words**

No question at this stage will say "Write all you know about X". And no question at this stage will ask you to deal with the whole of a subject or topic. It will direct you to look only at specific areas of it. Most topics you study will involve a number of key issues. They will also be related to broad underlying concepts or principles. Your reading, lectures and seminars should have highlighted these. If you look at them carefully enough the key words in a question will indicate to you which of these key issues or underlying concepts it wants you to deal with.

Example

'The centralisation of executive power in the hands of the Prime Minister since 1979 was primarily due to the personality and style of Mrs Thatcher'. How far do you consider this to be true?

The question is asking you to look at a number of specific things. (Some things are explicitly mentioned. Others are just suggested).

- **the centralisation of executive power in the hands of the Prime Minister** suggests you describe and explain what executive powers are now in the hands of the PM. (Before you can do this you also need to explain what you understand by **executive powers**).

- **Since 1979** suggests you need to show how the present situation is different from that existing pre-1979

- **due to the personality and style of Mrs Thatcher** asks you to explain how the **personality** and **style** (NB what do you mean by "style"? Not her dress-sense!) brought about the changes. In dealing with this part of the question you would need to refer to specific situations in detail as well as making broader generalised comments.

- **How far this statement is true.** A good answer to this section would be a long one - possibly a third of the essay - because it would consider what **else** led to the **centralisation of executive power in the hands of the Prime Minister** from 1979 to the present day. Only then would it be possible to asses how far Mrs Thatcher's **personality and style** caused it to happen.

Dealing with the issues identified by the key words in this way would generate a perfectly adequate answer to this question, although you may well end up not dealing with the issues in this order

Problems

● Identifying exactly what the question wants you to do is not always easy. **The key issue words may need interpreting** before they help you to answer the question.

A not-so-simple example

Discuss the extent to which government policy on the sale of council homes has been successful in Anyborough District.

Government policy on the sale of council homes is easy to deal with. And in **Anyborough District** suggests you deal with how far the policy was successful only in that District.

Successful, however, needs interpretation. Before you can judge the **success** of anything you need to identify what its **aims** were. So you need to consider these, concentrating on those that have since proved important or controversial and ones that will therefore be central to your argument later. Only after you have dealt with the **aims** can you consider how far these aims have been achieved.

● You can now generate an essay plan from this

- ■ **describe**   Government policy on the sale of council homes
- ■ **explain**   what you consider its aims were
- ■ **consider**   what happened in Anyborough District that fulfilled these aims
- ■ **consider**   what happened in Anyborough District that didn't fulfil the aims
- ■ **discuss**   the overall success of the policy. This is your conclusion.

- However, before you can really get to grips with the essay you have to **analyse the aims** - you need to break them down into **different types of aims**.

  The difference between a good and a mediocre essay in answer to this question will depend partly on how you do this, how comprehensively you interpret **aims.** Obviously the main aim of the policy was to sell council homes. But it had broader aims too - social, economic and political (Your research will have identified what other broad aims it had). So when you consider the **success** of the policy you can deal with how far it fulfilled each of these.

  It is worth noting that in the minds of the people who devised the policy these aims were obviously inextricably bound up with each other, but they are much easier to discuss if you separate them out and deal with them separately.

- In addition to this, in your conclusion, you may want to interpret **successful** in a broader way, looking at the effect the success of the policy had on society as a whole, or on the subsequent fortunes of the government responsible. But this is a discussion for the conclusion, **after** you have dealt **in detail** with the issues specifically mentioned in the question

- You can see from this examples that interpreting the key word **successful** is the "key" to a "successful" essay!

This question has not been chosen at random.

How far do you think X has been successful (and, by implication, how far has it been unsuccessful).

or

Discuss the advantages and disadvantages of X

are very frequently found essay questions. They can usually be dealt with in the same way as this example.

● Very often the question will contain **key issue words that you don't recognise as such.** These tend to be words you take for granted because they are very familiar anyway, or ones which your lecturers have been using throughout the course. Not asking yourself what they **really** mean - not **defining your terms** before you start - can lead to fuzzy essays where the focus of the argument is not clear.

It's always worth looking at every word in the question and asking yourself "Is this word important?" and "What **exactly** does it mean?"

Another not so simple example

Is there any such thing as a typical Victorian city?

(The word **Discuss** is not used but it is implied in this kind of question)

This seems such an obvious question that defining your terms and analysing exactly what the question refers to seems unnecessary. However, if you first of all consider what - for the purposes of this essay at least - you mean by **city**, you will produce a much more focused argument.

At a very simple level cities are urban developments of a certain size. Identifying this (obvious) fact simplifies the problem right away by eliminating some places from your discussion.

If you then go on to define **city** in other ways it will actually help you to generate a plan for the whole essay.Consider the characteristics that enable you to recognise a city. There are things like the architecture of public buildings and types of housing, the industry and types of commercial organisation, the social composition and the geographical distribution of the classes, the administrative structure and its powers. These could well form the basis of your essay plan. You have, therefore, by defining in detail what you mean by a city, generated the **beginnings** of a plan for your essay - and you haven't started on the research yet!

! Two words of warning !

Defining your terms does not mean looking for a dictionary definition.

- The kind of **definition** you want is one that interprets what the term means in this context - in the context of the subject and the topic. Hence an interpretation of what it means to you as a student of the subject, and to experts in the field, is what you are looking for. You are likely to find it in your notes or in your reading - not in the dictionary.

- **don't over-define.** You have to use your judgement as to what words in the question are really important, and what are peripheral. Defining every word in the question leads to a long, tedious and, ironically often irrelevant essay.

● **If after doing all this you still don't know what the question is looking for**

  ● **discuss it with other students**

  ● **read some 'general introduction'- type material** like journal articles or general discussion chapters on the topic. Make some notes on ideas, approaches, angles. Don't bother about the detail yet.

  ● **read your lecture notes.** They may provide clues.

Step 5 : Do the reading and take notes

● **Remember the question and focus your reading and note taking on it.**

● **Identify each set of notes**

from books, with
- author, title, publisher, place of publication, date

from journal articles, with
- author, title of article, title of periodical, volume number, issue number, date, page

from lectures, with
- lecture title, lecturer, date

● This will take a long time. Getting books is never easy and reading/assimilating ideas and information is a time-consuming process. Start early.

● You may well end up with a lot of notes you don't use. Don't be tempted to cram information in anywhere just because you don't want to waste it!

● **When you have read as much as you think you need**

leave it for a few days if possible

- one day at the very least

Step 6: Gathering material for the essay

You may think you have already done this because you have done the reading and note-taking. But the books you take ideas from may well have been setting out to prove different arguments. **You** need to select ideas that relate to **this** essay and adapt them to **your** argument.

First of all you need to collect together all the ideas you think may possibly be relevant.

● **Brainstorm**

● **Write down all the relevant ideas you have in your head - in brief note form.**

Don't worry too much, whether the ideas you are collecting 'fit' the question and your approach to it. Just brainstorm.

There are a number of reasons for doing this

- You need to select the best ideas to suit the question. You can only do this if you have a lot to choose from.
- There is always a tendency to think of things as you are writing the essay -and put them in when you think of them, whether they 'fit' there or not! Putting all your ideas down first at least helps to get rid of that problem.
- You will be concerned, when writing the essay, to remain in control of the direction of your argument. This often leads you to leave important things out if you can't quickly think of a way to make them 'fit' at the time you think of them. If you have done the thinking beforehand you stand a chance of covering a wider range of ideas and keeping the structure clear.

● **Then go through your notes and pick out all the other ideas you find there that you may want to use.**

Write down ideas, theories, examples, details - anything you think might be useful - in brief note form. There is no need to write them all out again in detail.

● **Then leave a gap of at least 24 hours**

You need time to assimilate the ideas

before you can select and organise them.

Step 7 : Organise the main stages of the argument

You now have two starting points from which to construct your essay.

- A plan generated from an analysis of the essay question.

- A collection of ideas (in brief note form) that will help you develop the argument suggested by the plan.

- **Now put them together to form the main stages of the argument.**

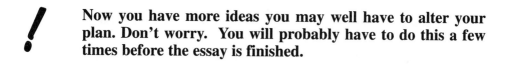

Now you have more ideas you may well have to alter your plan. Don't worry. You will probably have to do this a few times before the essay is finished.

- Look at the latest plan and identify the main stages of the argument. Write down each one as a heading on a different sheet of paper.

- Decide which of your brainstormed ideas are related to the main stages of your argument and write them down on the relevant sheet of paper.

- **Reject the rest now !**

- If you find there are some stages of your argument you have no ideas for read some more. This time concentrate **specifically** on the material that is missing. You are trying to fill gaps in your knowledge - not rethink the whole subject.

Step 8 : Break down the subject into its main topic areas

Most subjects that you will be asked to deal with at this stage are complex. They will involve a large number of inter-related issues. If you don't identify these and separate them out in order to discuss them you will end up in a hopeless muddle.

● **Break down the subject, into its major issues and separate them out in your mind.**

If there are a lot of issues you may have to select only the most important or interesting ones for discussion. These issues will provide you with part of the basic structure of your essay.

Exactly where in the essay-writing process you do this will vary. The main issues will probably emerge as you do the reading but you really do need to identify for yourself exactly what they are before you start planning your argument in any detail.

Example

Describe and discuss the advantages and disadvantages of current provision for 16+ students in the Scottish state education system

Education provision for 16+ students in the Scottish state education system is an impossibly large subject to deal with in its entirety. You need to decide first of all what different types of 16+ education exist - what **different kinds of provision** exist. (There is a lot of difference between them so you'll probably need to deal with them separately). And, before you can discuss their relative advantages and disadvantages you need to decide what distinguishes one form of **education provision** from another. To do this you need to identify basic features that may be different. These may include

- **the objectives**

- **the curriculum content**

- **the range of teaching methods**

- **the methods of assessment**

You can then deal with **each of these in turn** in relation to **each of the providers.**

Of course they are, in reality, all inextricably linked , but it is much easier to deal with each one adequately if you deal with them separately and then show how they are linked.

Step 9 : Organise each main section

● **Look at each main stage of your argument in turn.**
This is easy if they are on separate sheets of paper.

● **Pick out the main ideas.**
Leave the details, the evidence that proves your point, the examples, and the minor points till later.

● **Put all related ideas together.**
Make sure that each main idea is thoroughly explained.

● **Put all the main ideas into a suitable order.**
What order this is will vary but putting the most important first will usually serve the purpose well.

● **Look again at your interpretation of the question.**

● **Look at the main stages of your argument. Check each one relates to the question and, together, they answer it.**

● **Add introductory and final sentences to each section**

● Make sure each main stage in the argument has an introductory sentence. It acts like a heading and if you are writing in report format will be replaced by a heading.

● Essays don't have internal headings but the reader still needs some other form of direction signal to indicate where a new stage of the argument begins. So an introductory sentence is necessary.

● Add a final sentence that relates back to either the introductory sentence of this section, or to the question.

Step 10 : Add the detail

● **Every point you have made needs to be proven by use of evidence**

Academics in different subject areas have different definitions of what constitutes evidence in their particular subject. But some general things can be said about how a point in an argument can be backed up in order to convince the reader.

● You can use

- examples
- quotations
- the results of case studies
- data in the form of figures
- diagrams
- tables
- graphs
- anything that is appropriate to the subject you are discussing

● But this evidence cannot stand alone Simply quoting or referring to corroborative evidence is never enough.

● **First make the point.**

● **Then quote the evidence.**

● **Then explain how your evidence proves the point you are making.**

Example

(This extract from an essay refers to the novel , *The Go-Between*, by L. P. Hartley).

One of the major themes of the novel is the danger and destructive power of sexual passion. The book sets out to show how Leo, the narrator and central character is the victim of this power. However, Hartley cannot make this idea explicit to the reader because his narrator is a young adolescent who is not yet consciously aware of sex. He is disturbed by his own latent sexuality, and by that of the two characters he is closest to, but he cannot explain the cause of his feelings. Hartley, however, needs to be able to convey the cause to the reader. One of the ways in which he does this is by using the belladonna plant as a symbol.

> The shrub... topped the roofless walls, it pressed into their crannies, groping for an outlet, urged on by a secret explosive force that I felt would burst them (p191)
>
> The sullen heavy purple bells wanted something of me that I could not give (p191)
>
> Torn between fascination and recoil I turned away (p129)

Here the writer of the essay has used the quotations to "prove" the fact that the belladonna plant is being used as a symbol to convey an idea. But they don't, on their own, "prove" anything at all.

The writer needs to add an explanation of **how** the quotations prove the point being made. This could be done by pointing out that many of the words used to describe the plant have sexual connotations. This would involve an explanation of the connotations of a number of key words. Comment is also necessary on the fact that Leo's feelings in relation to the plant are ones more usually associated with a sexual relationship. And again specific expressions that illustrate this would need to be extracted and commented on. This would then "prove" the point that the plant is being used symbolically to reveal Leo's latent sexuality.

But it still hasn't dealt with the point that these quotations convey the idea that sexual passion is "dangerous and destructive". To do this comment would be needed on the way words with sexual connotations are used in conjunction with words suggesting danger and destruction. Only after having done all this would the writer have "proved" the point. Then the "other ways" in which the idea is conveyed would need to be dealt with.

- Every kind of evidence needs the same kind of treatment. **Graphs or tables,** for example, **need to be followed by an explanation of what they demonstrate.** It is not enough simply to leave readers to draw their own conclusions.

You need to discuss things like

- The implications of the data you quote
- The different possible interpretations of the data you have used
- The conclusions to be drawn from the data you quote and a
- The implications of this case study's results for other situations.

/ **When lecturers say you haven't developed your argument enough it is this stage you have not done sufficiently thoroughly. If you are doubtful about how to use evidence find an easy-to-read textbook in your subject and concentrate on how that author uses evidence to prove his/her point.**

Step 11 : Divide each main stage of the argument into separate paragraphs

● You should now find that each main stage of the argument has a number of separate major points in it, backed up by minor points and reinforced by a number of pieces of evidence. The essay will be much more readable if **each of these major points is put into a separate paragraph.**

A more detailed description of what constitutes a paragraph - and what doesn't! - is included in the **Presentation** section.

● Each of these paragraphs should have an **introductory sentence** too. But this sentence will only link it to the preceding paragraph.

Step 12 : Check

The main body of your argument should now be ready for writing up.

● Check

- ● Does each stage of the argument have a **general statement at the beginning?** It should introduce this stage of the argument and also relate directly to the question.

- ● Does this stage of the argument contain a number of ideas, **all developed in detail?**

- ● Are all **related ideas grouped together?**

- ● **Is everything relevant?** Check that you have not started to develop some minor point in a way that is not relevant to the point you are making at this stage. It may well be interesting. It may fit in at some other point. But if it does not relate directly to the main point of this part of the argument leave it out.

- ● Is each point you have made **backed up by evidence?** The evidence should have been discussed so that you explain to the reader **how** it proves the point.

- ● Is there a **final sentence** that relates back to the introduction to this stage of the argument or back to the question itself?

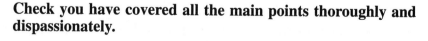

Check you have covered all the main points thoroughly and dispassionately.

At this stage nobody should be able to tell if you disagree with any of them! That comes later.

Step 13 : Write the Introduction

At this late stage this sounds like very odd advice. But if you try to do it any earlier it is likely to be much more difficult - or a failure! You can't introduce what you are going to say and the order in which you are going to say it until you've actually worked this out. You probably won't have worked it out until you reach this stage.

Some people can plan an essay in their head so completely that they can write the introduction first. But they are unusual. Most people can't.

- **The rules for writing Introductions to academic essays are simple -** and very different from those for other kinds of writing.

  - **Don't waffle!** An introduction should tell the reader exactly **what** you are going to do in the essay - related to the question you have been asked to discuss.

  - It should **explain how you are going to argue**. It will not tell the reader what you are going to say but will highlight the issues you are going to discuss and the order in which you are going to deal with them.

  - This may involve **discussing what you are not going to deal with** as well. Sometimes key terms are so broad in their reference that you cannot possibly hope to cover all their implications. You need to choose the main ones - and **explain why** you chose these and rejected others

  - You may have to define key terms. Don't do it by using dictionary definitions. You may be able to do it by giving your own interpretation of the words. More often you will need to give explanations that have been worked out by other people. Books, articles, critical essays - things like this -are the best sources of "definitions" of the key terms to start essays with.

  - A **second introductory paragraph** is often necessary to explain **the background** to the subject or to identify basic assumptions you are making but which you are not going to consider in the essay.

  - You may want to begin with something that **arrests the reader's attention** a quotation or an apparent paradox or an interesting fact. But this is a frill and should be no longer than a sentence or two.

- The style of the introduction is very important. Essays have different types of introduction from reports. **They should read almost like a summary** of everything except your conclusion.

Example

With reference to the transition from feudalism to industrial capitalism critically analyse the relationship between at least three of the following components : mode of production, family and household, urbanisation, population structure, violence, mechanisms of social control.

One possible - and perfectly acceptable - introduction to this essay is

There have been many views on the transition from feudalism to capitalism, differing largely over the causes and timing of this change. There are a few dissenting voices that trace continuity from the 1980s to medieval times but most writers are unanimous in agreeing that great change did occur. The three components in this change which I will look at are the mode of production, population structure and the mechanisms of social control. The approach I will use will be to take each these individually and describe the changes that occurred, and then take them together and identify the relations between them.

This version makes a general, but relevant, introductory comment and then goes on to say how the essay will tackle the subject and in what order. This is exactly what an Introduction should do.

This version, however, sounds like the introduction to a report with the subheadings removed and turned into sentences. It has, in the process, become personalised. Academic essays should avoid this if at all possible. That doesn't mean your Introduction should sound pompous or ultra-formal. Nor should it be verbally embroidered unnecessarily. Nor should it become vague and unspecific about what the essay is going to do.

The second version is just one way of improving it as far as style is concerned.

Views on the transition from feudalism to industrial capitalism vary. The differences of opinion mainly centre on the causes of the change and its timing. There are some dissenting voices who see it as simply one step in a process of continuous change from the Middle Ages to the present day but most writers agree that great change did occur. Three of the most important components in that change were the mode of production, the structure of the population and the mechanisms of social control. Important though they were individually, however, they did not operate independently. The relationship between them was also significant in bringing about this most fundamental of changes in society.

Step 14 : The first 'final' draft

 Don't attempt to write the Conclusion yet.

● **Write a rough draft of the final essay**

At this stage everything, except perhaps the opening and closing sentences of each main stage in the argument, will probably be in note form, on separate sheets of paper. Some people will be able to write the final essay from these notes but most students find they need to do a rough draft of the essay at this point. When this is completed you will be in a good position to write your conclusion.

● **At this point have a break**

- preferably 24 hours

Step 14 : Write your Conclusion

!

- **The Conclusion may well be a quarter or a third of your essay and be largely responsible for what grade you get.**

- **Don't confuse the Conclusion with the short final flourish that rounds the essay off. They are different things.**

Conclusions cause problems - usually because you are tired by this point in the exercise.

But it is often the most important part of the essay . So do have a break before you come to write it.

● **Reread the question before you write the Conclusion.**

Check you are still tightly focused on what it asks you to consider.

● **Exactly what the Conclusion contains will vary according to the question you are answering.**

● **If the question asks you to make a judgement between differing or opposing views or theories**

The earlier parts of the essay will contain descriptions and explanations of these different views. Your Conclusion should then be the place to make your judgement and justify it - in detail and with as many reasons as possible. This may well take up a large proportion of the essay.

If you have been unable to decide that one view or theory is better than the others there is nothing wrong with a conclusion which says so. This can be the mark of an honest essay, and even of a very good one, provided that two other things have been done. First, you must have reviewed the evidence completely, and secondly, you must have shown why it is difficult to reach a definite conclusion.

● **If the question asks you to decide how far you agree with a given proposition**

The early sections will contain explanations of all the issues to be taken into account and all the possible approaches to them. Actually answering the question 'to what extend do you agree' is done in the Conclusion. Because you have to explain why you think as you do, relating it to everything that you have described previously this will take up a considerable amount of the essay.

● **If the question asks you simply to discuss a proposition**

This is the point at which you need to consider the arguments more generally. Perhaps this will involve discussing this issue in relation to basic principles, or looking at it from a different point of view or to put it into a broader context.

● **If the question asks you to make suggestions or recommendations in the light of a previously described situation**

These suggestions will require lengthy treatment as well, and will form your main conclusion.

● **If the question simply asks you to explain or describe**

The conclusion will be short. You only need to highlight the most significant points and make some general comment. Even in this case, though, it is not enough to tack on **Thus it can be seen that .....** followed by information already given. However, this kind of essay is rare in higher education.

Step 16 : Last paragraph

- **Write a short generalising paragraph,** relating back to the question rounds off the whole essay.

    - You can test its effectiveness by asking whether it would tell a reader who had skipped all the rest:

        - what the original question was.

        - what your answer to it is.

    - It may also be appropriate to introduce an interesting new thought or you may want to put the whole subject into a wider context - but don't start on a whole new line of argument.

Step 17 : Final draft

- **Before you start this, check**

  - **the length.** If you need to cut it, it will probably be in the early sections where you are laying out the facts of the case, or giving background information. Check that the description and explanation don't outweigh the discussion

  - **the balance of the argument.** Is the Conclusion long enough? (See **Step 15**). If it isn't, check to see you have considered enough issues and given reasons for your judgements. Lack of balance is a major source of problems with essays.

  - you have stuck to answering the question and not wandered off into **irrelevance.**

  - every point has its **"proof"**

- **You may need to do a second draft**

- **Don't carry on redrafting**
  You will start to generate errors and confusion out of panic or boredom!

● **Now leave it at least 24 hours -**

preferably longer

Step 18 : Edit it - at least twice

This is a painful exercise. Everyone hates it because the essay never seems as good in the morning as it did the night before! And it's too "new" for you to contemplate changes.

But often simple changes can make the difference between a mediocre essay and a good one. The best plan is to leave it a couple of days before you edit it or get someone else to do it for you. They **must** be sympathetic, honest and have an interest in the subject. You are, after all, writing essays for "an intelligent but uninformed colleague".

- **Revise it twice - for different things**. You can't concentrate on the overall flow of the argument if you're checking the spelling at the same time.

  - **Revision 1**

    Check

    - **the argument is focused** on the question throughout

    - the argument flows **logically**

    - there are **explicit links between the main sections** of the argument

  - **Revision 2**

    Check
    - **sentence structure**

    - **word choice** - does it say exactly what you meant it to say?

    - **spelling**

    - **quotations and references** - have you identified the source?

    (These are all dealt with in **Section 6**).

You have now finished your essay!

- Before you hand it in make a copy of it

- Just before you are due to get it back marked, reflect on how it could be improved.

- In the meantime reflect on how you could adapt this method to suit your needs better next time you write an essay

SECTION 3

REPORT WRITING

The uses of reports

In many ways the process of writing a report is very similar to that of writing an essay. There are, however, some important differences in the purposes for which they are used.

● **The Report form is often used for**

- **recording** - the findings of a feasibility study or survey.

- **describing** - an experiment and drawing conclusions from it.

- **investigating** - a problem or situation, with recommendations for its solution.

- **analysing** -   work done
  the implications of a sequence of events
  the effects of implementing a proposal.

- **considering** - a series of different proposals.

- **assessing** - the workings of a system and how it might be improved.

- **evaluating** - an organisation against a set of new guidelines.

● **The purpose of a report can be to**

- **inform** readers about a system or situation and to put forward a series of possible recommendations as a basis for discussion.

- **predict** the consequences of implementing different proposals (always on the basis of past experience, and taking current trends and circumstances into consideration).

- **persuade** the reader   to take a particular course of action

                                       to adopt a plan

                                       to agree with a point of view

(In this situation it is still desirable that other courses of action/plans/points of view will be considered, if only to be dismissed).

 These purposes - especially the first two - have a lot in common with essays. They examine all the options and come to conclusions just as discursive essays do.

The writing process

The process of deciding on the nature of the task, collecting and selecting information, and constructing the argument is similar to that of essay-writing.

There are differences, though, and these mostly lie in

- **the preparatory work**
- **some elements of the structure**
- **the layout**

Preparatory work

The basic nature of the preparatory work is the same but there are some differences. You usually don't start with a question but with a set of terms of reference or instructions about exactly which area of a subject is to be investigated. If you are not given these then your first task is to decide exactly what you are going to do.

- **You need to know, before you start work**

  - **what your specific objectives are**

    - exactly what subject area you are covering
    - exactly what you are trying to find out
    - exactly what the limits of the study are
    - what the relevant issues are
    - what degree of detail you need to work to.

    If you can make your own decisions about this it is important to choose carefully. It is always better to choose a remit that is within the bounds of reasonable possibility and do it really well. Leave wide investigations for your PhD!

- **what your more general aims are**. What kind of response do you want from your reader - agreement with your evaluation, for example, or approval of a proposed course of action? Or are you simply providing a series of proposals as a basis for discussion?

- **who your readers are**
  - what degree of knowledge they have already
  - what background information they will need
  - what opinions they have already
  - how familiar they are with technical terms and the procedures involved in the area you're dealing with
  - what style of writing they are likely to find both comprehensible and appropriate.

- **what methods of investigation you are going to use**

  - a literature search (reading all the books already written on the subject!)
  - structured or unstructured interviews
  - questionnaires
  - on-site observation
  - experimentation
  - any other method

The structure

● Fundamentally this is the same as for a well-constructed essay. The major differences are

　● the inclusion of a Summary at the very beginning, before the Introduction.

　● the nature of the Introduction.

　● the division of the main body of the report into obviously separate sections.

　● the separation from each other of Conclusions and Recommendations.

The basic reasons behind the differences are that

　　● reports are intended to be easily read and absorbed.
　　● they should allow readers to focus only on what most interests them without reading the whole document.
　　● they give readers a clear idea of the findings, conclusions and recommendations before they start to consider the detailed argument.

● The following **structure** is a very commonly used one but you must find out if this is acceptable in the department you are writing for as some have a favoured house-style.

1　　**Title** - This should be informative rather than brief . If it needs three lines use three lines! But try to arrange them so that the reader is led from the general to the particular.

2　　**Summary** - This is a vital part of all but the very shortest reports. It gives readers a quick review of the findings, conclusions and recommendations before they read the detail.

3   **Contents list** - The main sections and sub-sections of the report and the pages on which the reader can find them are listed at the beginning of the main body of the report. This also gives the reader some idea of what the report has to say.

4   **Introduction** - It should

- give **the background** to the report
  - what situation gave rise to it
  - why it is necessary
  - why the work was done
  - what the problem was

- **state the terms of reference** - the aims and objectives of the report

- clearly explain **the ground that will be covered** and **why** this has been selected

Two other things may be necessary depending on the type of report being written

- explain **what similar work has been done in the past**, or is being done at the moment

- **outline the methodology**. This may be
  - an explanation of the kind of research you undertook (with your reasons for doing it in this way)
  - an explanation of where you got your information from and why this source was selected
  - a comment on any gaps in the information that may affect the conclusions

5   **The main body of the report** -   (This is not the heading for this part of the report). It will almost certainly be the longest part because it consists of the investigation, findings and discussion. It will therefore need dividing up into sections and you need to devise headings to indicate the various stages of the discussion or investigation.

Be particularly careful at this stage that all your section headings are of a similar level of generality

Example

The report on a comparison between two courses in the same subject run at different Universities may well have sections on

- **Course Structure**
- **Course Content**
- **Method of Delivery**
- **Method of Assessment**
- **Level of Credit**

These are all broad subject headings under which a number of different issues can be dealt with. If another heading were to be included

- **Examinations**

this would not be appropriate because it is only one method of assessment and so should be subsumed under that heading.

One note of warning. When you have divided up your investigation into sections and allocated all your material to the various sections, you may well have some material left over. If this happens it may well be that

- you have omitted it from one of the Sections
- you have divided up the Sections inappropriately
- it is not central to your argument anyway

6   Conclusions - Here the report sets out clearly what the conclusions are. This will mean repeating statements that appeared in the previous section. But the reader will not want to have to go back to find these. S/he wants them clearly set out all in one place. Conclusions (which relate to the present, however, should be separate from Recommendations (which relate to the future). For example, the **conclusions** to be drawn from a consideration of how council estates are run could be that decision-making is delayed and costs more because of tenant involvement. The consequent **recommendations** could be that tenants should be informed of decisions only after the event (!).

7   Recommendations - Again this section may well repeat what has already been said in the main the body of the report.

8   Appendices - These are a much mis-used part of many reports! The acid test is to ask yourself what information the majority of readers will need to enable them to understand and be convinced by your reasoning. This information should be in the main body of the report. Diagrams for example are usually more useful close to the text they support rather than buried in an Appendix. Anything else, especially if it is lengthy or very detailed, should go in an Appendix or a series of Appendices. This may result in the Appendices collectively being longer than the report. In certain situations this may well be justified.

9   Glossary of Terms - The non-specialist who has to read the report may need an explanation of some of the technical terms. If there are only one or two such terms, explanations could be done by a note early on in the main body of the report.

10   Bibliography - This will be the same as for essays.

The layout

● **Each section of a report should have headings and subheadings and a classification (numbering) system.**

You can use numbers, upper and lower case letters and Roman numerals in various combinations

Examples

   ■   2.1.1.   ■   A 3 i)
         2.1.2   A 3 ii)
         2.1.3   A 3 iii)
   ■   2 b i)   ■   II c i)
         2 b ii)   II c ii)
         2 b iii)   II c iii)

The first example is probably the most commonly used now but it doesn't really matter what numbering system you use. The important thing is that it should be consistent.

● **Lists within the report need care**

If you have to list things within the report make sure that all the items in the list are expressed in a similar way. If, for example, you are making a list of actions to be carried out in a survey make sure they all take the same form.

Example

1.1   **Check** for water leaks
1.2   **Identify** faulty taps
1.3   **Location** of old lead piping

The first two begin with an instruction and the third one doesn't. A better form would be

1.1   **Check** for water leaks
1.2   **Identify** faulty taps
1.3   **Locate** old lead piping

The style

The style of a report is only different from that of an essay in that, because of the system of headings and classification of information, the introduction of new points will be less wordy. It all still needs to be written in **continuous prose** - not note form.

● **Write in straightforward language you are familiar with**.

Impressive-sounding words and phrases are no more appropriate in reports than they are in essays. In both they usually sound pompous and - more importantly - they obscure your meaning. Technical language is necessary and important but avoid jargon.

● **Be aware of your intended audience**.

The target audience for a report may significantly affect the language used. Clearly a report on tenant management co-operatives for prospective members would be written in a different style from one for senior housing department managers.

● **Write directly.**

The aim of a report - as with an essay - is to communicate your meaning as quickly and effectively as possible.

● **Avoid expressions such as:**

It can be seen in Figure 4 that X increases more sharply than Y
This solution is indicated by the findings.

● **Use**

Figure 4 shows that X increases more sharply than Y
X increases more sharply than Y. (Figure 4)
The findings indicate this solution.

SECTION 4

STYLE

The importance of style

Obviously the content and structure of your essays are by far the most important things about them. But style and presentation make an enormous difference to how well they are received.

A variety of styles is acceptable in academic writing but some styles are better than others, and certain things are taboo. Exactly why one style is "better" than another and what the "best" styles are could keep a seminar group occupied for some considerable time! However, a good general principle is to use a style which allows you to convey exactly what you want to say as clearly as possible and in a way that does not distract the reader.

What you are saying should be the focus of any reader's attention, not how you are saying it.

Advice about what style to use in academic essays usually includes the word **impersonal**. This does not mean that your writing should be dry and totally devoid of personality. If your writing sounds like a government document it will probably send the reader to sleep! However, it should avoid the two extremes of colloquialism and excessive formality. The essay should not sound like casual conservation, sales-talk, executive jargon or a legal document. What this means in practice can be encapsulated in a few simple suggestions.

Styles to avoid

- ## colloquial phrases

  These are phrases like   ✗   **mind you**
                         ✗   **let's face it**
                         ✗   **what on earth**

  They add a lot to conversation but they are out of place in formal writing

- ## clichés

  These are expressions that have been used so often they have lost virtually all meaning. (Some of them had very little meaning in the first place!) They include expressions like

       ✗   **in this day and age**
       ✗   **at this moment in time**
       ✗   **avoid them like the plague!**

- ## dialect words and grammar

  Dialect words are ones that are only used in certain areas, and are only comprehensible to the people in those areas. They are always associated with conversational speech - in fact they are responsible for much of its liveliness. However, they are out of place in essays and reports that are intended to be universally comprehensible to all English-speaking people.

  Dialect grammar is dealt with in some detail in **Section 6.**

- ## slang

  This is another group of words and expressions that adds colour and vitality to speech. But they are words that tend to be used by certain groups of people, and only for a short period of time before they go out of fashion. They are not therefore suitable for writing which is intended to be read by a wide variety of people at an unspecified time

- ## abbreviated forms like it's, haven't, can't, shouldn't.

  Again they are an vital element in all forms of speech, but not suited to academic writing. Also avoid abbreviations like **eg, ie, etc.**

- ## hyperbole

  This is the technical term for verbal exaggeration.

  > ✗   **It was a total wreck**
  > ✗   **There were thousands of them**

  People use it, not to deliberately mislead, but to add colour to their statements.
  In a context where accuracy and careful consideration are the prime considerations hyperbole is out of place.

- ## jargon

  Whole books have been written on what this is but most people can recognise it when they see it.

  All subjects use words which are only comprehensible to people familiar with that subject. They are technical words, used to express specific, subject-related ideas in a kind of shorthand. They are essential because they give you the tools with which to consider the subject.

  Jargon is different. It involves the use of words specific to a certain subject, profession or activity which are **intended** to be incomprehensible to people in general. Fashionable "executive" phraseology comes into this category as well.

  > ✗   **as a resultant implication**
  >
  > ✗   **downsizing (or rightsizing!)**
  >
  > ✗   **expedite completion**

  There is a perfectly reasonable, much more universally comprehensible alternative to all jargon phrases. The reasons it is used are many, and are of varying degrees of legitimacy! For academic purposes jargon is simply not appropriate, because your aim should be to communicate ideas, not obscure them.

● excessively scholarly words

These are in fact, a kind of jargon.

In earlier centuries Latin was the language of learning. When English took its place it inevitably absorbed a large number of the Latin words used by scholars who had previously written in Latin. Many of these words have since become basic to the study of many academic disciplines. They have become, in effect, similar to technical terms.

- **epistemological**
- **euphemistic**
- **polemic**
- **isochronous**

However, many others have largely dropped out of use. They are only used now by writers who have a particularly strong attachment to them for aesthetic reasons or by people who are trying to impress readers with their erudition. Your aim when writing essays is to convey ideas. Using words which draw attention to themselves rather than clarifying the message you are trying to convey is therefore not a good idea.

● unnecessary wordiness

- ● Sometimes, for example, essay-writers use **two descriptive words which mean much the same thing.**

    ✗ **The language used is vague and unclear**

- ● Sometimes words are included as a **kind of embroidery.** A phrase is used where a word would do.

✗	due to the fact that	=	✓	because
✗	on account of	=	✓	because
✗	at the present time	=	✓	now
✗	with regard to	=	✓	about

Worse still, a phrase containing "long" words is used where one simple word would be better

✗	to conduct an investigation into	=	✓	to investigate
✗	to give some assistance to	=	✓	to help
✗	to arrive at an estimation as to how much	=	✓	to estimate

All these things have a tendency to make your writing appear "woolly". They make it seem that you are having difficulty getting to the point.

- To avoid the same kind of impression one revision of your finished essay should be focused on places where you have simply said **the same thing twice** in slightly different ways. (As a rule the second attempt is usually the better one!)

- ## words you find by looking them up in a Thesaurus

The words you find as alternatives to the one you originally thought of are rarely exact equivalents and can serve to confuse the meaning completely. They may also be perfectly all right as words but out of place in that particular context. You have no way of knowing this unless you are familiar with them and their usage beforehand.

- ## any words or phrases you do not completely understand.

This will lead to your writing unintentional nonsense. And one piece of nonsense will outweigh three pages of sense in the mind of the reader!

- ## dogmatic statements

Unless you are prepared to give unequivocal evidence to prove your point, these are very dangerous.

✗   **The author means that........**

You have no way of knowing what the author meant -unless you have been in personal contact, or that author has made a public confession as to what s/he meant. It is therefore truer to say

✓   **The author seems to be suggesting that......**

● **over-long sentences**

These can arise from a number of causes.

You can have a sentence made up of too many bits (clauses), all dependent on each other. Readers may well forget the first part of the sentence by the time they have reached the last part. They then have to reread it to ensure they have understood it all. This rereading prevents them from appreciating the logical flow of your ideas.

The sentence may contain too many long phrases. This tends to happen when, (to make sure you have covered all the angles), you qualify important words so much   that the impact of the original word gets lost. Once again readers can't follow it without rereading.

The style you should use

- Your writing should be aimed at an imaginary person - **an intelligent but uninformed colleague** (unless the task you have been set specifically asks you to do otherwise).

- Whoever you are writing for, however, you should aim to convey your thoughts as **clearly and accurately** as possible.

- Your other aim should be **impersonality without pomposity**

  - Express your ideas **directly**. (This is probably the best way of doing it).

    ✓ **The tests should be modified**
    ✓ **H is longer than G**
       or Fig 6 shows that H is longer than G.
    ✓ **The conclusions to be drawn from this enquiry are as follows.....**

  - **Use** expressions like

✓	**it seems that**
✓	**it appears that**
✓	**it is a good idea to**
✓	**it is vital that**

    They are all better than   ✗ **I think**

  - Use a **discursive style** rather than an instructional one. This book is meant to be instructional so expressions like **you should do this** or **do not do that** are appropriate. An essay, on the other hand, is a discussion, so instructions are out of place.

  - Use **sentences of varying length**. However, remember that long sentences - more than 20 words - may sound elegant (if you construct them correctly!)but they are more difficult to understand at first reading.

The problem of "I think"

There is a long-standing tradition that **I think** is an inappropriate expression in academic writing of any kind. (Some departments don't mind it as much as others). There are various ways of getting round the problem and some of them are just as bad as **I think** if not worse!

Avoid

✗   I - as in **I think** or **I believe** - at least until you reach the Conclusion of your essay.

✗   **We** - as in **We can see that.....** or **We arrive at this conclusion by......**.

This may be used by lecturers (who presumably assume that everyone in the group is coming to the same conclusions at the same time!) but it is inappropriate in essays and reports where there is only one author.

✗   **Pompous expressions beginning with It**, such as

It is recommended that the tests are modified

It can be shown that H is longer than G.

✗   **The writer**, as in

The following conclusions are drawn by this writer

✗   **You** to mean people in general

You would find this difficult to understand.

✓   It is better to express it directly

People find this difficult...

This is difficult to .....

Expressing your ideas directly as suggested at the beginning of this section should make all these expressions unnecessary.

SECTION 5

PRESENTATION

Presentation

Obviously the content of your work is by far the most important thing about it. Beautiful, even artistic, presentation will not compensate for a poor quality argument. However, the presentation of your work is important. In any case some markers penalise poorly presented work very heavily. (It can, in fact, help you to improve the quality and clarity).

Most departments issue guidelines to their students at the beginning of the course as to how they want work presented. It is important to follow these. Losing marks for not doing as you are asked in something as simple as this just has to be accounted stupidity!

The following guidelines may prove useful if you are not presented with alternative ones.

Graphical presentation

Word processing/typing

Your work should be laid out as follows.

On white A4 paper

On one side of the paper only.

Use 1 margins at the bottom and on the right; 1.5" margins at the top and on the left.

Use 1.5 spacing

Use at least a 10 point font as the norm. You can use a variety of other fonts for specific purposes, but use them consistently and only when necessary. Don't use them for decorative effect!

Indent paragraphs. Your work is easier to read in this format.

Check for typing errors - especially if someone else has typed it. They are surprisingly frequent

One very important thing to bear in mind when using a word-processor is that, because you can only see one screen at a time, it's difficult to structure your essay using only the screen images. It is much better to get a hard copy early on in the essay-writing process so that you can see the whole thing in order to move bits around as necessary.

Handwriting

- Write neatly. It has been suggested that if your writing is easy to read a marker will assume it is worthy of an A until it has proved otherwise. If it is illegible it will be assumed to be worthy of only a very low mark until it has proved otherwise!

- Use A4 paper, wide lined and write on one side of the page only.

- Margins provide space for your tutor to write comments on the essay, as well as enhancing its legibility. So leave a margin on both sides of the page

Writing Conventions

- If, during the course of your essay, you need to refer repeatedly to something with a long title it is acceptable to abbreviate it. The most intelligible way of doing this is to write the whole thing out the first time you use it and put the initials you are going to use subsequently in brackets afterwards. After that the initials will suffice.

  - **The Equal Pay Act, 1970 (EPA) dealt with issues such as......**

- Numbers under 10 are usually written as words **unless** they are being used as statistics or dates when they are written as figures. Percentages are represented by the symbol when they occur with a number!

- Avoid using abbreviations such as **eg** or **ie** or **etc**. Write the first two out in full. And never use **etc**. It means **There must be more examples but I can't remember/be bothered to think of them at the moment!**

The Title Page

The front cover of your work should carry the following information.

Example

Title: (written in full) Discuss the role of the Senior Civil Servant and the degree to which he can influence the legislative process

Student's Name: James Oak

Course Title: Politics

Tutor's Name: Dr M Osborne

Date Submitted: 6 December 2001

Using and presenting evidence

Using evidence

The section on developing your ideas deals in some detail with how to incorporate evidence into your argument and how to use it to justify the point you are making. This one deals with the sources of that evidence and how to present it.

Using other people's ideas.

In most academic essays you will need to use other people's ideas. Your essay should not be made up solely of other people's ideas but, if you are going to discuss a subject from different angles and different points of view, if you are going to deal with different interpretations of a text or different reactions to a situation, or if you are going to evaluate different people's concepts or theories, you are going to have to refer to other people's work. To justify your own views you will also need to refer to work done by other people in the form of statistics, case-studies, experiments and facts of different kinds. Inevitably much of this will come from books but there are two important things to remember.

- Books are not the only source of information and ideas. To begin with, they are often not published until a year after they are written. Often, therefore, they are not a good source of **up-to-date** information. Periodicals or even, in some circumstances, newspapers are better for this. The same is true of radio and TV documentaries. In addition to this the most relevant and useful information can often be gleaned by interviewing people who are involved in a job or activity - people with experience. And your own experience, where relevant, is useful too. "Evidence" comes in many forms and from many different sources.

- Just because something is stated in a book - or a periodical, documentary or official document - it is not necessarily "right". Judgements may well have been overtaken by events. Facts may be out of date. Figures may be wrong. Interpretations of data may well be based on false premises. Conclusions may be biased by the author's philosophy or political viewpoint. Before you use ideas or information, therefore, you need to have thought about them and come to a judgement as to whether they are likely to be unbiased, accurate and up to date.

Acknowledging Sources

When you do decide to use ideas or information taken from other people's work you need to acknowledge the fact. Acknowledging the fact that an idea comes from someone else is easy: deciding exactly what to acknowledge is not so easy.

If, for example, you are dealing with a subject you knew little about before you started researching it every idea will be someone else's. You could therefore end up with acknowledgements on every line, which is tedious to read.

It is also sometimes not easy to identify exactly where an idea came from. It may have been planted in your mind some time ago and is now so much "yours" that you can no longer remember the source. Much of our knowledge falls into this category.
So what do you acknowledge? It is difficult to make hard and fast rules about all this but there are a number of guidelines you can follow.

Acknowledge the source when

- you are going to use an idea or theory as the basis of your argument
- you quote information from an obvious source
- you use statistics, results of experiments or case-study material
- an idea obviously sprang from the work of one person or where it is unique to one writer

You don't need to acknowledge the source of an idea if it is

- a matter of common knowledge
- used by most lecturers or writers on a subject and they don't acknowledge the source

You should be able to pick up a more accurate sense of what to acknowledge from your reading. Observe how other authors do it.

Remember too that ideas can be original. They don't always need the backing of a reference to be valid. They **do** need, however, to be justified or proved.

Using Quotations

- The most common reason for using **quotations** is as support for a point you are making. In themselves they **don't prove anything**. They simply suggest that your idea has the backing of someone else, or was, in fact, someone else's idea originally. In any case the idea itself **always needs explaining**.

- **The quotations should almost always be short.** If you quote too much your own argument will get drowned or your essay will look like a patchwork of other people's ideas held together with a few of your own words.

- The other main reason for using quotations is to refer to a text which is, in itself, the subject of the discussion.

In both cases the graphical conventions are the same.

Types of quotation

- **An indirect quotation** is where you summarise the writer's ideas and incorporate them into your own sentences. This is the most appropriate way of referring to what another author has said. This is because it is much easier to make the idea fit your argument if you put it in your own words. You need to be careful, however, that you don't alter the sense of the original in your paraphrase.

  This kind of quotation does not need inverted commas because you are not using the other author's words. But it does need the source of the idea identifying at the point in the text when you use it.

- Smith identifies three stages of development - the initial, medial and terminal (1986, p3)

- Three main stages of development are identified - the initial, medial and terminal (Smith, 1986, p3).

● **A direct quotation** is where you use the author's actual words. This kind of quotation is most appropriate when the author has expressed the idea so well you couldn't improve on it or when it is the way the idea is expressed that is the important point about the quotation. It needs to be laid out somewhat differently.

When the quotation is one sentence or less enclose the quoted words in inverted commas and incorporate the whole quotation into a sentence of your own.

- Montgomery suggests that, "Maintaining a separate ethnic identity does not, however, depend necessarily on maintaining a totally distinct language" (1986, p 80)

(If you want to omit the **however** in this quotation leave it out and replace it with **...**)

If the quotation is longer it is still incorporated into a sentence of your own and still enclosed within inverted commas. The quoted words, however, are put on a separate line and indented from both sides. The introductory words are separated from the quotation by a colon as well.

- Montgomery goes on to give an example of this:

  As a group they (Afro Caribbean Black Britishers) probably have a more marked sense of ethnic separateness than at any time since the 1950s. Where this is marked linguistically it is not necessarily by using a distinct language but by a denser use of Creole forms with Caribbean origins (p80).

Note that if you need to explain vague words like "they" you can put the explanation in square brackets and italicise it to show these are your words, as in (Afro-Caribbean Black Britishers).

Quotations should not interrupt your argument, but be made part of it. They should always be introduced in incorporated into a sentence.

Quotations from literary texts

The graphic conventions for quoting prose passages from literary texts (novels, essays) in literary essays are exactly the same as quoting from other kinds of texts.

If you are **quoting frequently from one text** you only need to refer to the author and the date the first time you reference it. (After that a reference simply to the page will be enough).

- The narrative viewpoint of *One Day in the Life of Ivan Denisovich* (Solzhenitsyn 1963) appears to be that of Ivan himself. Sometimes the narrative actually lapses into the first person: "Now our column had reached the street" (p103)

If you are **quoting from a play** then you should refer to the title, the Act, the scene and the line(s). (After the first reference the title can be omitted).

- Hamlet's disgust for the world is often expressed in images of sickness and decay. The heavens, for example, are a "Foul and pestilent congregation of vapours" (*Hamlet* Act 2, 2, 305-6), not a "majestical roof fretted with golden fire" (Act 2, 2, 304). Denmark is "an unweeded garden/That grows from seed, things rank and gross in nature/Possess it merely" (Act 1, 2, 135-137).

When you are **discussing individual words and phrases**, or listing phrases you want to cite as examples, each individual word or phrase has to be enclosed in inverted commas. (There is no need to keep referencing the text, unless the point at which these words occur is significant).

■ In fact Hamlet's speech at this point in the play (Act 3, 4) is full of expressions conveying disgust - expressions such as "making love over the nasty sty", "the bloat king", "paddling in your neck", "a pair of reechy kisses", and "the fatness of these pursy times".

When quoting extracts from poetry or verse drama it is normal to **preserve the line divisions** of the original if the quotation is at least two lines long.

■ The final lines of the poem are deliberately anti-climatic:

Yanked above hounds, reverting to nothing at all,
To this long pelt over the back of a chair

If it is shorter, but runs over a line division, it is more sensible to **mark the division with a diagonal line.**

■ The expression "a grasped fistful/Of splintered weapons" is a good example of Ted Hughes's alliterative technique in this poem.

Using statistical data

Very frequently the evidence you cite to prove a point will involve quoting statistics. There are several different ways of doing this and it is important to choose one that is suited to your specific purpose.

The first thing you have to do is to consider how useful it is going to be for the reader. You need to look at:

- whether the information is really **related to the point** you are trying to make - or is it just intended to impress the reader!

- if the data is **valid**. You need to consider things like whether it is up to date, from a reliable source or relating to relevant dates.

- what exactly you are **trying to show**

- what **presentation method** would make it easiest for the reader to pick out the relevant information

- what **narrative** you will have to include to explain the significance of the data

Presentation methods

Some presentation methods are more useful for academic purposes than others. Useful ones include

Tables

They have certain advantages.

- They present figures obtained from research in an **orderly** way. (It may be your research or someone else's).

- The fact that the figures are presented in an orderly way enables the reader to **locate actual figures quickly** and to compare different sets of data with each other. It is also possible to **identify patterns** within the figures.

- They give the reader access to the **details of the actual figures** from the original research data. Readers can therefore draw their own conclusions, and check the validity of your comments on them.

But before a reader can get all this out of a table it needs:

- an **explanatory heading** that mentions all the significant factors included in the table

- very carefully considered **column and row headings**

- the **salient points highlighted** in some way

- a **narrative explanation of** the significance of figures. Readers should not simply be left to draw their own conclusions. These conclusions should be an essential part of your argument - or the table was not necessary to the essay in the first place!

Average gross weekly earnings, excluding the effects of overtime: full-time employees on adult rates, 1973 -1987

Great Britain **Pounds per week**

	1973	1975	1977	1979	1981	1983	1985	1987
Women	22.6	37.4	51.0	63.0	91.4	108.8	125.5	147.2
Men	37.5	60.8	78.6	99.0	137.0	163.5	190.4	222.1
Differential	14.9	23.4	27.6	36.0	45.6	54.5	64.9	74.9
Women's earnings as a % of men's	60.3	61.5	64.9	63.6	66.7	66.6	65.9	66.3

Source: New Earnings Survey

The earnings gap between women and men is much greater when weekly earnings are considered instead of the `pure' measurement of hourly pay-rates excluding overtime. Even when men's greater opportunities for overtime are discounted, the earnings gap is greater for weekly than for hourly earnings because of men's longer working hours.

The earnings of women in full-time employment improved (though not steadily) relative to men's earnings until the early 1980s. subsequently an earnings gap of just over a third has persisted between female and male full-time earnings.

(Source: HMSO, (1988) **Women and Men in Britain : A Research Profile**, p47 (edited)

Fig 1

- It is important not to make tables more complicated than the reader needs to understand the point you are making. For example, you may have a table which details annual figures over a period of 30 years say 1900 to 1930. If you are primarily interested in **trends** over this period, and the trends follow a fairly predictable pattern, it may well be best to quote figures in five year intervals -1900, 1905, 1910 .... In this way the trend is easier to see quickly. In the example (fig 1) the writer has used two yearly intervals because there are more significant inconsistencies in the trend in certain years. This kind of simplification is not always appropriate.

- The important consideration when using tables is always what the reader can get out of it, not how much you can get into it.

Bar Charts

These are not as detailed or precise as tables but are often more useful for showing one thing in relation to another. They can be horizontal or vertical.

- **They enable the reader to make quick comparisons between two or more things - size or quantity for example (fig 2).**

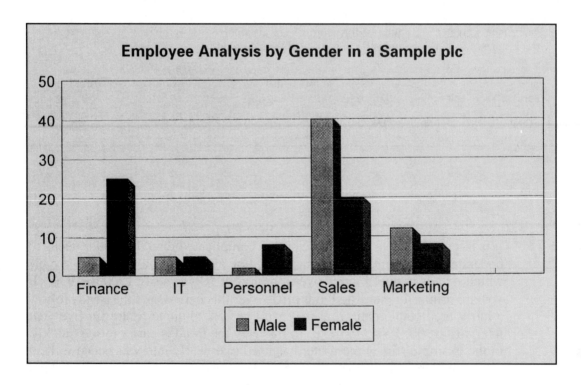

Fig 2

- They can also show clearly **changes in quantity over time (fig 3).**

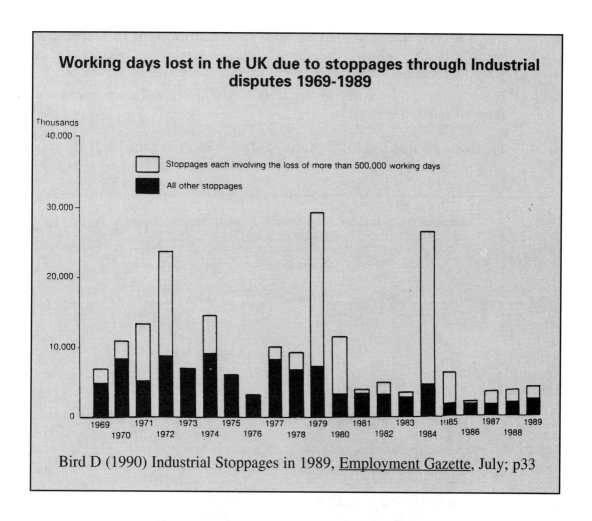

Working days lost in the UK due to stoppages through Industrial disputes 1969-1989

Bird D (1990) Industrial Stoppages in 1989, <u>Employment Gazette</u>, July; p33

Fig 3

- They too need to be followed by a **narrative explanation** of the factors you want to draw attention to.

Pie Charts

- These are very useful in showing **how each component of a situation relates to the whole**. The size of each segment of the `pie' reflects the size of the component it represents in relation to the size of the whole. The 360° of the circle represent the whole - 100% - and each segment is proportional to this (fig 4).

- Pie charts are **not useful if statistical precision is required.**

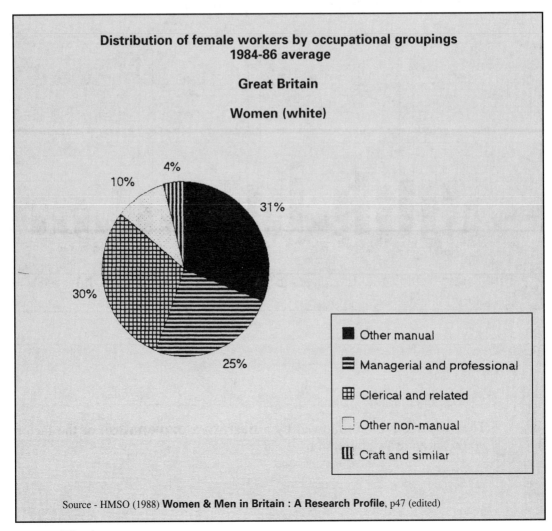

Fig 4

Graphs

- Graphs are of most use in giving an **impression of a trend.**

- In designing a graph it is important to remember that the main thing a reader will pick up is the shape. So you need to ensure that it is a **suitable pictorial representation of the situation it illustrates.** The number of divisions on each axis should therefore be in proportion to each other so that the graph line doesn't give a false impression.

- Multi-line graphs like fig 5 are useful for **comparing one trend against another**. Too many lines however, need to be avoided they simply give an impression of muddle. In this respect, how effective is fig 5, for example?

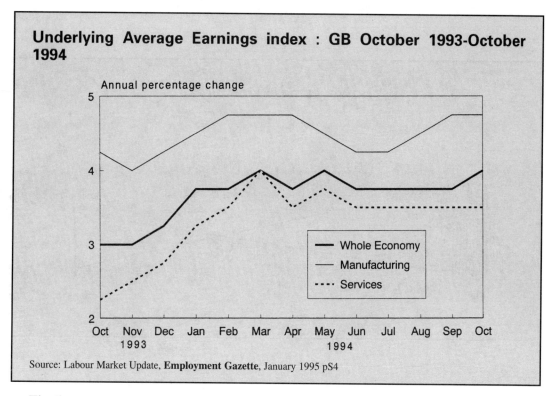

Fig 5

- Graphs are not suitable for presenting readers with an accurate picture or detailed figures.

Diagrams

Sometimes one small diagram can explain things more clearly than a whole page of text.

They are especially useful for picturing

● **objects and how they work.** The diagram here will be a simplified representation of what they look like.

● **operations and mechanisms you can't see.** In this case the diagram is a model of the process that makes it easier to envisage as in fig 6

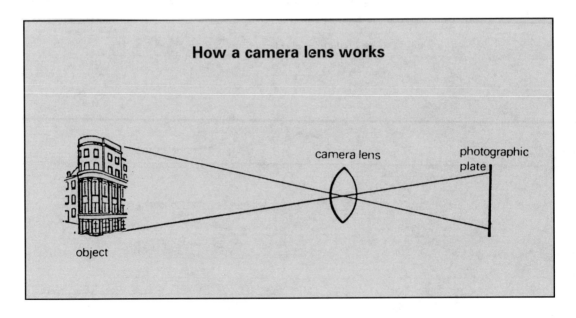

Fig 6

● **Any hierarchical structure** can be represented by **a tree diagram**

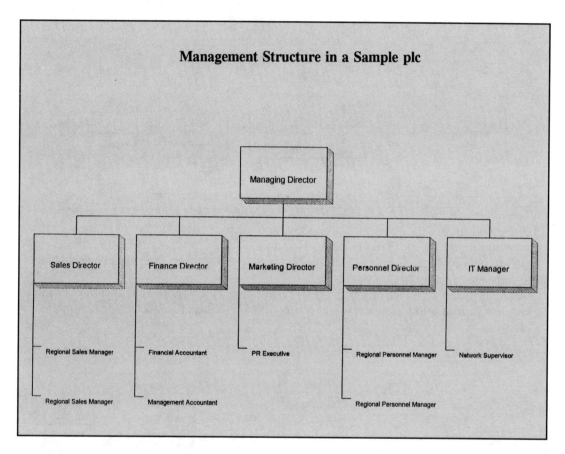

Management Structure in a Sample plc

Managing Director

Sales Director | Finance Director | Marketing Director | Personnel Director | IT Manager

Regional Sales Manager | Financial Accountant | PR Executive | Regional Personnel Manager | Network Supervisor

Regional Sales Manager | Management Accountant | | Regional Personnel Manager

Fig 7

- **Any chronological series of events**. Is best represented by a flow chart

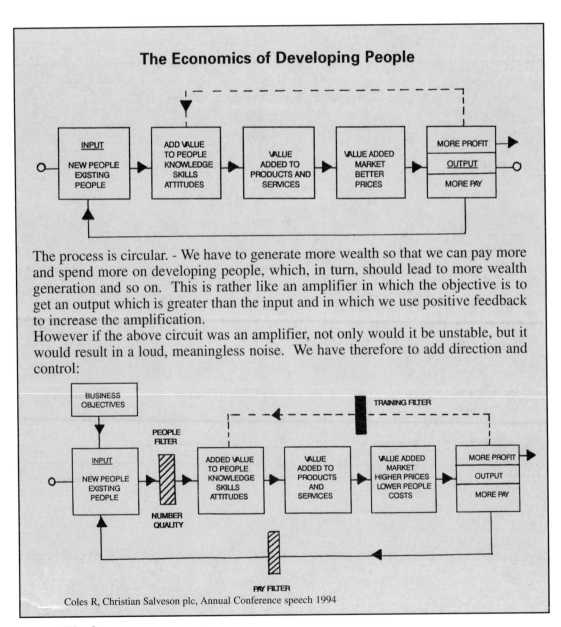

The Economics of Developing People

The process is circular. - We have to generate more wealth so that we can pay more and spend more on developing people, which, in turn, should lead to more wealth generation and so on. This is rather like an amplifier in which the objective is to get an output which is greater than the input and in which we use positive feedback to increase the amplification.

However if the above circuit was an amplifier, not only would it be unstable, but it would result in a loud, meaningless noise. We have therefore to add direction and control:

Coles R, Christian Salveson plc, Annual Conference speech 1994

Fig 8

- Note the way in which these two diagrams have been inforporated into the text. The narrative does not supply repeat the information contained in the diagrams. It comments on the significance of it.

- **Getting across the** fundamental principles of concepts and theories as in fig 9

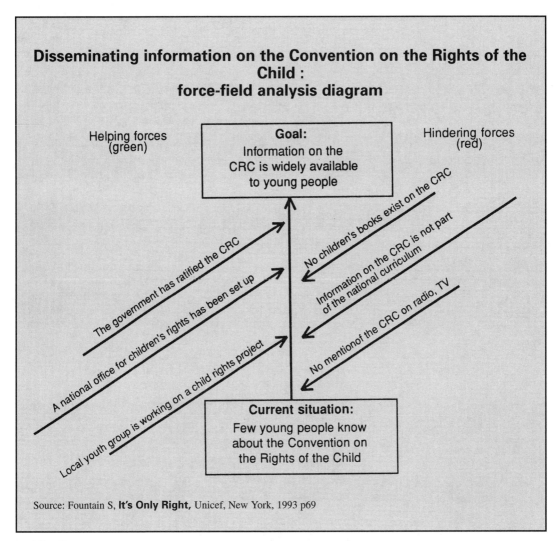

Fig 9

- Don't be tempted, however, to use diagrams when simple explanations are just as good. This gives the impression you are trying to stretch your material, or, worse still, patronising your readers!

- Remember, just as with statistical data and quotations, diagrams should be followed by an explanation of what they imply in relation to your argument.

Referencing
and
Bibliographies

Referencing

Whatever form your evidence takes you need to identify the source so that anyone reading your work can check the accuracy of the facts or ideas you have referred to. It also helps them judge how well you are relating what you have read to your own argument and how well you relate fact to theory.

Different departments in different Universities often have very firm ideas about how they want you to acknowledge the source of an idea or piece of information. You will also find a whole range of different ways of doing it in the books you read - footnotes, chapter-end notes, or a reference list at the end of the book are three of the most common. In the absence of other instructions, however, there is a very simple, yet clear way to do this. It involves two stages

- refer **briefly** to the source of the material in the body of the essay

- give all the publication details of the book in a Bibliography at the end

The brief reference in the body of the text can be done in two ways

- **Burnett (1978) reports that demographers believe the cause of the population explosion must be ...**

- **As Smith argues in his commentary on policing:**

   the confidence of society is greater the closer it is to its local police force. We should therefore welcome —— the scaling down of large scale metropolitan units (Smith, 1962, p212)

If you use these methods this is all you need to do at this point because the Bibliography at the end of the essay or report will contain the rest of the necessary information about the book.

Bibliographies

At the end of your essay or report you should provide a bibliography which lists **in** alphabetical order of authors' surname the reading material which you have referred to in your essay **and** anything which may have provided useful background information without being specifically referred to. Your bibliography should provide details of title, author, date, and all the relevant publication details. These vary with the type of publication you are using but they should always be designed to enable a reader to find the book or article easily.

There are **numerous** ways of laying out these publication details. Different publications do Bibliographies differently from each other. The graphics are different in type-script, print and hand-writing. The conventions vary from country to country. In addition to all this each University department may also have different preferred styles!
It is important, therefore, to ask the lecturer you are writing for if s/he has a preferred style. In the absence of any other guidelines, however, the following ways of presenting the material in a Bibliography would be acceptable in most cases.

For books by one author or written jointly by a number of people

- Burnett, J., (1978) *A Social History of Housing, 1815-1970*, Methuen, London.

- Jones, B. and Johnson, R., (1990) *Making the Grade: A study programme for adults*, Manchester University Press, Manchester.

  The date **can** be put at the end.

- Keneally, T., *A Family Madness*, Hodder and Stoughton, London, 1986.

In handwritten scripts or when you are using a machine without an italic or bold facility you just underline the title of the book.

- Burnett, J., (1978) <u>A Social History of Housing, 1815-1970</u>, Methuen, London.

The author's name(s) and the date can be written on the line above all the other details, in upper case letters.

- **BURNETT, J., (1978)**
  A Social History of Housing, 1815-1970, Methuen, London

For chapters by one author in books written or edited by another

---

- Glucklich, P., (1984) The Effects of Statutory Employment Policies on Women in the UK Labour Market, in G. Schmid, and R. Weitzel, *Sex Discrimination and Equal Opportunity*, Gower, Aldershot.

- Altmann, S A., (1987) "Private Communication", in B M., Mayor, and A K., Pugh, (ed), *Language, Communication and Education*, Croom Helm, Beckenham, Kent.

Note that the chapter title may or may not be enclosed in inverted commas.

For publications with no named author

- UNESCO, (1965) *World Illiteracy at Mid-century*, Paris.

- Department of Education and Science, (1991) *Higher Education - A New Framework*, Cmnd. 1541, HMSO, London.

For articles from periodicals, journals and newspapers

- Osborne, M J., (1988) Access courses in mathematics, science and technology: selected case studies, *Journal of Access Studies*, 3.2, pp. 48 -63.

- Wortman, S., (1976) Food and Agriculture, *Scientific American*, Sept. Vol. 6, pp30-0

- Bronfenbrenner, M., "Japan Faces Affluence", *Australian Economic Papers*, Vol. 24, No. 38pp 16-44

- Osborne, M J., Cope, P. and Johnstone, R., (1994) The backgrounds and experiences of adult returners to an Access to Secondary Teaching scheme, *Continuing Higher Education Review,* 58, 1/2, pp. 41 - 63.

- Meikle, J., "The Glass Ceiling", *Education Guardian*, 31st May 1994

Note that you don't need to give the publisher and place of publication when giving the details of periodicals, journals or newspapers, but that different periodicals number each issue differently. You need to give the details relevant to the publication you are using.

Note also that the article title may or may not be enclosed in inverted commas.

SECTION 6

THE MECHANICS OF
ESSAY WRITING

Before you read this section try to answer the following questions

If you get all, or most of them, correct you don't need to read the rest of the section

Self-assessment questions

The following extracts contain examples of English that is unacceptable in formal writing - though many of them would be perfectly acceptable in informal conversation.

For each extract

1. **Identify the error and underline it**
2. **Briefly explain what is wrong with it - in whatever way you can.**

---

1. Only 1% of children under the age of 5 are in local authority day nurseries (Neville, 1990, p4).

    Unfortunately workplace creches are considered by the government to be a taxable benefit. This increases their cost to employees significantly.

    Women who want to return to work after having their children are therefore unable to find affordable childcare.

    This is one of the biggest problems faced by working mothers and one of the major factors influencing their achievement of equal opportunities.

    It is, however, a problem caused by the government's social policy and therefore beyond the scope of the Sex Discrimination Act.

2. Conditioned responses have been extensively researched. Pavlov's famous experiment with dogs, for example.

3. The factories were owned by the bourgeoisie. The capitalist, rich middle-class who had recently come to power.

4. Some people blame aggressive behaviour on lack of discipline at home and in school. While others attribute it to the influence of violence in films and television.

5. Interest rates are bound to rise. The reason being government policy.

6. Pensioners facing an inevitable reduction in the interest on their savings.

7. There are still far more men in promoted posts than women, for example only 20% of secondary heads are women.

8. However, we cannot conclude that voting according to class and family values are a feature of the Scottish electorate alone.

9. This version of the play had been previously wrote in folio manuscript form.

10. Individuals adapt their language to the context in which they are using it. They speak and write different according to the situation they are in.

11. The book ends by a universal pairing of the main characters.

12. This kind of behaviour is kept within the confounds of society.

13. This work questions the fundamental principals of nuclear physics.

14. The people in the sample have been broken down by age and sex.

15. Through tribunals women could use the Equal Pay Act 1970 to claim equal pay. The problem of the non-existence of a man carrying out the same or similar work was overcome when the Equal Pay Act was amended.

16. Social mobility has created many problems - lonely old people, no sense of community, young people not enough carers, young parents with no external support.

17. The writer uses repitition as a device for highlighting key ideas.

18. It is neccessary to seperate the two groups completley.

19. To say definately whether this is the case is not possable.

20. Their was a flaw in they're argument.

21. Most individual's use aggressive behaviour as a survival mechanism.

22. It's function is not clear.

23. Peoples reaction to violence has been tested in a number of studies.

24. The writer described the water as ghostly and corpse-like.

25. These results haven't been replicated in subsequent studies.

26. Texts differ according to academic content eg. methodological, empirical, philosophical etc.

27. In this day and age such assumptions can no longer be made.

28. How can this situation be resolved? Let's face it, we can start by reducing numbers.

29. This proposition is weakened insofar as there is more hypergamy and hypogamy at the elite level in the most differentiated societies than in societies of intermediate differentiation.

30. It is necessary to be especially careful with regards to an increase in numbers.

Identifying the problem

The following pages

1   Give the correct version of each statement

2   Identify the problem in each case

The rest of the Section makes suggestions as to how you can avoid making similar errors. The pages dealing with the problem are referenced after the correct version.

- This section does not deal with all these problems comprehensively. It will **not**, for example, attempt an exhaustive explanation of the grammatical system of the English language. It will, in fact, try to avoid using grammatical terminology as far as possible.

- What it **will** do is explain how to avoid the most common errors - the ones that have the most negative effect on the reader. It is important to eliminate these because they grate on the nerves and divert attention from **what** you are saying to the irritation they cause with **how** you are saying it.

- The suggestions are, in each case, just **one** way of avoiding the error - not the only way. It has usually been chosen because it is the easiest or most reliable way.

Answers to self-assessment questions

1.   The paragraph has a number of errors. (The suggested improvements have been printed in bold).

Only 1% of children under the age of 5 are in local authority day nurseries (Neville, 1990, p4). **(At this point add details of other forms of child-care available and the numbers of children being catered for by them. Emphasise the fact that most forms of child-care are expensive. Then proceed to the next point about work-place nurseries - but don't start a new paragraph because you are still discussing the same subject).** Unfortunately workplace creches, **(which should be of enormous benefit to working mothers,)** are considered by the government to be a taxable benefit. This increases their cost to employees significantly. **(No new paragraph here because the next sentence is about the same subject).** Women who want to return to work after having their children are therefore unable to find affordable childcare. **(No new paragraph here. What follows still relates to the same point).** This is one of the biggest problems faced by working mothers and one of the major factors influencing their achievement of equal opportunities. **(No new paragraph here. The next sentences simply links the point you have been making with the subject of the essay).** It is, however, a problem caused by the government's social policy and therefore beyond the scope of the Sex Discrimination Act.

See **Paragraphs**   Page 120

2.   Conditioned responses have been extensively researched - in Pavlov's famous experiment with dogs, for example.

See **Afterthoughts**   Page 123   ✓

3. The factories were owned by the bourgeoisie - the capitalist, rich middle-class who had recently come to power.

    See **Afterthoughts**   Page 123 - ✓

4. Some people blame aggressive behaviour on lack of discipline at home and in school, while others attribute it to the influence of violence in films and television.

    See **Unfinished sentences**   Page 125 - ✓

5. Interest rates are bound to rise because of government policy.

    See **Statements containing -ing words**   Page 127 - ✓

6. Pensioners are facing an inevitable reduction in the interest on their savings.

    See **Statements containing -ing words**   Page 127 - ✓

7. There are still far more men in promoted posts than women. For example only 20% of secondary heads are women.

    See **Sentences without full stops**   Page 129 ✓

8. However, we cannot conclude that voting according to class and family values is a feature of the Scottish electorate alone.

    See **Mismatch between parts of a sentence** Page 131 - ✓

9. This version of the play had been previously written in folio manuscript form.

    See **Dialect forms**   Page 132 - ✓

10. Individuals adapt their language to the context in which they are using it. They speak and write differently according to the situation they are in.

    See **Dialect forms**   Page 132 - ✓

11. The book ends with a universal pairing of the main characters.

   See **Using the Wrong "Little" Words**   Page 134

12. This kind of behaviour is kept within the confines of society

   See **Malapropisms**   Page 138

13. This work questions the fundamental principles of nuclear physics.

   See **Confusing pairs of words**   Page 135

14. The people in the sample have been categorised according to age and sex.

   See **Ambiguous words**   Page 138

15. Through tribunals women could use the Equal Pay Act 1970 to claim equal pay. There was a problem, however, when there was no man doing a similar job with which they could claim equality. This problem was overcome when the Equal Pay Act was amended.

   See **Overcompression
   of meaning into too few words**   Page 139

16. Social mobility has created many problems. This is mainly due to the fact that communities have been fragmented and family members separated from each other. This causes isolation, especially amongst the most vulnerable groups. Old people are particularly at risk because, as members of their peer group die and they become more frail, they become more dependent on external support. This was traditionally provided by the younger members of the family. If this family no longer lives in the same neighbourhood then loneliness is almost inevitable. Children and young people are similarly vulnerable groups, but in different ways....

   See **Overcompression
   of meaning into too few words**   Page 139

17. The writer uses repetition as a device for highlighting key ideas.

   See **Spelling**   Page 140

18. It is necessary to separate the two groups completely.

   See **Spelling**   Page 140   ✓

19. To say definitely whether this is the case is not possible.

   See **Spelling**   Page 140   ✓

20. There was a flaw in their argument.

   See **Spelling**   Page 140   ✓

21. Most individuals use aggressive behaviour as a survival mechanism.

   See **Punctuation**   Page 147   ✓

22. Its function is not clear.

   See **Punctuation**   Page 147   ✓

23. People's reaction to violence has been tested in a number of studies.

   See **Punctuation**   Page 147   ✓

24. The writer described the objects under the water as "ghostly" and "corpse-like".

   See **Punctuation**   Page 147   ✓

25. These results have not been replicated in subsequent studies.

   See **Style**   Page 69   ✓

26. Texts differ according to academic content. Three different examples are methodological, empirical and philosophical.

   See **Style**   Page 69   ✓

27. Such assumptions can no longer be made.

   See **Style**   Page 70   ✓

8. How can this situation be resolved? Reducing numbers would be

one way of doing it.

See **Style**   Page 68

29.   This proposition is weakened by the fact that more women marry into a higher or lower social class in very hierarchical societies than in societies that are less rigidly structured.

See **Style**   Page 69 ✔

30.   It is necessary to be especially careful about increasing numbers.

See **Style**   Page 69 ✔

Correcting the errors

Paragraphs

If your essay is a continuous, undivided lump of text, it will be very hard for any reader to pick out either the shape of the argument, or any particular part of it.

/   **Essays need paragraphs**

● **Not all paragraphs will be the same length.**

A paragraph should be a meaningful division within the whole argument of the essay. Not all will be of equal length. Some will illustrate their arguments in more detail, or with more examples. Some things take longer to say. There can be no fixed rule for length. But paragraphs of over 300 words can be hard to follow and paragraphs of under 50 words tend to look scrappy.

● **Beware the tabloid press look**

Paragraphs in academic essays, unlike newspapers, normally have more than three sentences! If your paragraphs are short you are probably doing one of two things.

Either   you simply make a point each time without developing it. "Developing an argument" involves giving reasons for your ideas, providing evidence for them, going into detail, giving examples, explaining **how** the examples prove your point, and discussing the implications of your ideas.

Or   you are not putting all related ideas together in one paragraph.

(The extract in Question One of the **Self-Assessment Questions** is an example of both these problems combined).

● Paragraphs need to be linked

The first sentence in each main section of the argument needs to be linked explicitly to the introduction and, hence, to the question.

As well as this all the paragraphs within each main section should be linked to each other explicitly. This explicit link can often be made by using one of the following words

- **However**   means that what comes next is somehow opposed to, or an exception to, what came before.

  - **However, the situation in Somalia is very different.**

  Do not use **However** to mean 'and', or just to decorate the beginning of a sentence.

- **Although**   means that what you have just said in the last paragraph is a justified qualification of the main point but does not invalidate it. It is followed by a statement of what the key important point is.

  - **Although all this is true, and early signs of growth are apparent, the important thing to note is that the economy is still in decline.**

- **Despite**　means that what you have just said in the last paragraph may seem to contradict the main point but it does not in fact actually do so.

  - Despite all this, the current situation shows signs of improvement.

- **Because (of)**　means that what you have just said in the previous paragraph is the cause of something and that this `something' would not be the case without it.

  - Because of this, many problems have arisen.

- **Therefore, so**　both mean that what follows is a consequence (logical or practical) of what has gone before. For example

  - Therefore, a change in patterns of employment seems likely.

They are all quite specific in meaning so don't use any of them to mean "and this is my next point which I think fits in here somehow but I am not sure how".

Sentences

For a reader to be able to judge how well you have grasped a subject and how well you can construct an argument s/he must be able to read it easily without having to stop too often to puzzle over the meaning. If there are too many hold-ups in the reading process the line of argument gets lost. It is important, then, that your sentence structure is accurate. Badly constructed sentences are very difficult to understand and they divert the reader's attention from what you are saying. If you know you have problems with sentences it's important to put them right **now.**

Within each paragraph each sentence marks a unit of sense. Between the opening capital letter and the final full stop comes a group of words which should have the following properties:

- **it should make sense**
- **it should sound complete**

Many people have problems with sentences. Some kinds of problem are very common and this Section attempts to deal with some of them.

Afterthoughts

- When people talk they often make a statement, realise it was a bit too vague, and then add a bit more to make it clearer or more specific.

  ■ **Could you come a bit earlier? At six o'clock perhaps?**

  The second statement is, in fact, an afterthought.

  If you write this down instead of saying it the second statement sounds unfinished. (There is no verb). In speech this doesn't matter but it is considered wrong in writing. So, in writing, these afterthoughts are attached to the end of the first statement by means of a dash.

  ✓ **Could you come a bit earlier - at six o'clock perhaps?**

● Afterthoughts are often used in essays to introduce examples, but if you punctuate them incorrectly they simply appear to be incomplete sentences. They need to be joined to the main statement by means of a dash.

■ **Texts differ in academic content - methodological, empirical and philosophical, for example.**

● Other kinds of afterthought are dealt with in the same way.

✓ **The factories were owned by the bourgeoisie - the capitalist, rich middle-class which had recently come to power.**

 Another way of introducing examples, is to put them into a separate complete sentence on their own.

■ **Conditioned responses have been extensively researched. Pavlov's famous experiment with dogs is one example.**

Unfinished sentences

- Sentences are often made up of two or more statements. Some examples are

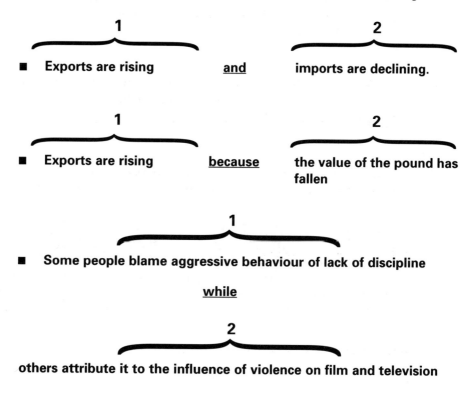

- Usually **the different statements are joined by a linking word.** They have been underlined in the examples -

and
because
while

●   If these two statements were to be separated and made into different sentences, the one beginning with the linking word would sound unfinished.

X   ...... **and imports are rising**

X   ...... **because the value of the pound has fallen**

X   ...... **while other attribute it to the influence of violence in films and television**

All these are only parts of sentences and so they all need another statement joined to them to make them make sense and sound complete.

A general rule of thumb - but not a rigid grammatical rule - is that, in academic essays and other kinds of formal writing, a statement that begins with a linking word needs to be accompanied by another statement that doesn't start with a linking word. Only then will the sentence sound complete.

There are a large number of these linking words but some of the common ones are

and, but, or
because - and **since, as, for** when they mean **because**
in order to - and **to** when it means **in order to, so as to, so that**
while, whereas, when, after, before, as, till, until
though, although
if, whether, unless, in case

●   Note that it is perfectly normal for this "rule" to be broken in speech. And advertisers and slogan writers specialise in breaking it! Academic writing, however, shouldn't sound like informal conversation so all the sentences used should follow this "rule".

Statements containing -ing words

● Statements in academic essays must **sound finished**

- **British Rail are getting there - sometimes!**
- **The pound is falling on the foreign exchange markets.**
- **Women managers are being found more frequently in commercial organisations.**

All these statements sound finished. They are complete sentences. (Note that they are all short. In order for it to be a complete sentence it doesn't have to be long or complex).

● But some statements containing -ing words don't sound finished.

✗ The Electricity Boards generating power at the lowest possible cost

✗ Pensioners facing a reduction in the interest rates on their savings

---

A way of avoiding this kind of incomplete sentence is to ensure that all -ing words have is, are, was, were, will be, has/have been, **or** had been **with them to make them sound complete.**

- **The Electricity Boards** { have been / are generating electricity at the / were
  lowest possible cost.**

- **Pensioners** { were / are facing a reduction in the interest rates on / will be
  their savings.**

● Sometimes -ing words are fine on their own in a finished-sounding sentence.

 This had the effect of reducing interest rates.

 There are difficulties caused by producing energy cheaply.

These sound finished and complete because the -ing words are being used in a different way. They are perfectly all right.

● So a sensible approach to the problem is that if the sentence sounds complete just leave it alone! If it sounds incomplete them it is probably because the words going with the -ing word are missing.

● One very commonly misused -ing word - which is extremely irritating to the reader - occurs in statements like

 Interest rates are bound to rise. The reason being government policy.

The reason being

causes the problem because the statement in which it occurs is incomplete.

You could make it complete by treating the second statement as an afterthought.

 Interest rates are bound to rise - the reason being, government policy.

 But a far better way to avoid the problen is to avoid the reason being **altogether. Use** because **instead.**

■ **Interest rates are bound to rise because of government policy.**

Sentences Without Full-Stops

This is one of the most common errors of all.

 It's vital you remember that a comma will not link two complete sentences.

X There are still far more men in promoted posts than women, for example only 20% of secondary school heads are women.

X Within the novel, images of rejuvenation are a constantly recurring feature,they punctuate the narrative at very frequent intervals.

● Each of these "sentences" actually contains two complete statements.

■ **1** There are still far more men in promoted posts than women

2 for example only 20% of secondary school heads are women.

■ **1** Within the novel, images of rejuvenation are a constantly recurring feature

2 they punctuate the narrative at very frequent intervals.

 If one sentence contains two or more complete statements they must be joined by something. The most common way to join them is to use a linking word.

■ Within the novel, images of rejuvenation are a constantly recurring feature, <u>since</u> they punctuate the narrative a frequent intervals.

It is far easier - and far more effective - to separate the two statements into two different sentences. In this case they must be separated by a full-stop.

- Within the novel, images of rejuvenation are a constantly recurring feature. They punctuate the narrative at frequent intervals.
- There are still far more men in promoted posts than women. For example, only 20% of secondary heads are women.

In certain circumstances you could separate statements with a semi-colon or a colon. But if you are making this kind of mistake it would be better to concentrate on using full-stops. Don't complicate the issue by trying to use two unfamiliar punctuation marks.

If you have this problem and you find it difficult to decide where to put your full-stops, try using no commas at all for a while. Limit yourself to using fullstops only. This will make you really think about where they go and when a statement is actually finished.

Words

Using the wrong word form

Mis-match between parts of a sentence

● Most statements involve someone or something (the subject) doing, thinking, saying or being (verb).

- **The author <u>portrays</u> characters in conflict with themselves.** **(doing)**
- **The government <u>considered</u> the proposals** **(thinking)**
- **Euro Disney <u>announced</u> another net loss in the third quarter.** **(saying)**
- **The economy is in recession.** **(being)**

● Sometimes the someone or something is having something done to it

- **The trials <u>were conducted</u> in the US.**
- **The conference <u>was attended</u> by all the EC Heads of State.**

● **In every case the form of the verb should "sound right" with the subject.** You probably have no difficulty with this when the person or thing doing the action is mentioned first before the verb in the sentence. It is obvious that **the trials were conducted** is right because **trials** comes next to **were** and **the trials was conducted** would sound wrong in written work. However, when the someone or something (subject) is a long way away from what they did, thought, said or were (the verb) it is often easy to choose the wrong form.

X **However voting according to class and family values are not a feature of the Scottish electorate alone**

Highlighting the important word makes it obvious that **are** is wrong. It should be **is.** The reason why you may well use **are** in this situation is because the word closest to it is **values** and that would need **are.** If you think about it, however, it is the **voting** that is not **a feature of the Scottish electorate alone,** not the **values.**

Freud, more than many other psychologists, stress the importance of the subconscious.

This is wrong because it is **Freud** who is doing the stressing. So it should be

✓ **Freud, more than many other psychologists, stresses.........**

Dialect forms

● The language in different parts of Britain developed in different ways from the same roots. These language differences are preserved in speech - not only in accents, but also in vocabulary and grammar. Some of them are obvious because they are words that only residents in a particular area can understand.

■ **It's a scunner**   will not be readily understood outside Scotland.
■ **Don't mither me**   will not be readily understood by people either in Scotland, Wales or the south of England.

Even if you use these words in speech you will probably not use them in formal writing because they will not seem suited to the context. But some dialect forms are not so obviously dialectal and you may well use them in writing because of this.

● One group of particularly problematical dialect forms occurs in people's use of verbs - the words that indicate what is done, said, and thought.

■ **They <u>was</u> proved wrong**
■ **They had <u>went</u> the wrong way**
■ **The letter was <u>wrote</u> on Tuesday**

These examples are what you would normally expect to find in conversational speech because that is where they are found most frequently - and where they are appropriate.

●   Because most **writing** and **formal uses of speech** are intended to be understood by anyone who can speak English, regardless of where they come from, **the appropriate form is the one you will find in most formal texts written in Britain.**

✓   **They <u>were</u> proved wrong**

✓   **They had <u>gone</u> the wrong way**

✓   **The letter was <u>written</u> on Tuesday**

●   Another regional feature, not appropriate in formal contexts, occurs with the words that are often found with the verbs - adverbs.

■   **They speak <u>different</u> in different places.**

In formal texts these words usually need an -ly ending.

✓   **They speak <u>differently</u> in different places.**

Using the wrong words

The "little" words - prepositions

- English uses a lot of these. **In, at, by, with, from, into, to** are some examples. They usually occur at the beginning of groups of words

    - **at** the beginning
    - **for** the foreseeable future
    - **in** other words

    They are also found with verbs (doing, thinking, saying and being words)

    - **they rely on the weather**
    - **it consists of two parts**
    - **it ends with a ceremony**

    The problem with them is choosing the right one for the context.
    In **speech** the right word for the context and meaning will vary in different parts of the country and the world.

    - **I'm waiting on the post.**
    - **Move it off of the chair**
    - **I'll wait while five o'clock**

    The right word in **formal writing** may well be different.

    - ✓ **I'm waiting for the post.**
    - ✓ **Move it off the chair**
    - ✓ **I'll wait till five o'clock.**

- There are no rules for learning these. The best way to learn the right version for essay-writing is to **take note of the ones used in text books or to look them up** - in a good dictionary, or in books written for foreign learners of English - in the section marked **Prepositions**. (Foreign learners are taught the kind of English that native speakers use in formal writing. So books written for them are often a good source of information on this kind of subject. There a many of these. A good one is

    Swan, M., *Practical English Usage*, Oxford University Press, Oxford, 1980).

Confusing pairs of words

Many words in English sound similar but mean entirely different things according to how they are spelled. There are some you will come across a lot in academic writing. It is best simply to learn them and be careful to use them in the right contexts.

Some examples of ones that are commonly confused are

● **effect/affect**

Effect is **usually** found with the words **the** or **an**, or it is plural, **effects** (it is a noun).

- It had an **effect** on the economy.
- **The effect was** greater than expected.
- **Effects** such as this are common.

Affect (or **affects**) usually means **to bring about a change in something** (there is another meaning but it is not found very often)

- The acoustics **affect** the sound quality of the woodwind.

Effect can be used as a verb but it means **to bring something about** or **to make something happen**. It is often used with the word **change**.

- The manager really **effected a change** in the company ethos.

The confusion arises because **affect** means **to have an effect on**!

● **principal/principle**

Principal means **main** or **most important**. Used on its own it means **the most important person**.

- The principal awards degrees.
- The principal argument in favour of this policy is......

A **principle** is **a rule or basic law**. (Sometimes when the word is used in the plural - **principles** - its meaning is **rules of moral behaviour)**

- **The principle on which the system operates is ....**
- **It is a society where behaviour is based on very different principles from those we adhere to.**

● practice/practise

Practice is the noun - as in **a practice, the practice, many practices.** (One way of remembering it is to think of **ice** as a noun, also the name of a thing.)

Practise is a verb; it is what you do.

- **He practises every day.**

● compliment/complement

Compliment is a flattering remark, or the act of making a flattering remark.

Complement is something that completes something else - as in **the complement of the sentence**.

It can also be used as a verb to mean **goes well with, provides a satisfying balance to** as in

- **The two colours complement each other**

● discreet/discrete

Discreet means **prudent, careful about divulging information**

- **A civil servant must be discreet in the handling of sensitive information.**

Discrete means **complete in itself, self-contained**

- The department is a discrete unit, independent of the rest of the organisation.

● precede/proceed

Precede means **go before**

- A precedes B in the alphabet

Proceed means **go on** or **carry on**

- The essay is proceeding well

You need to be particularly careful about the spelling of these two.

● uninterested/disinterested

Uninterested means **not interested**

- He could not concentrate because he was uninterested.

Disinterested means **able to take an objective and unbiased view of something**

- He was not involved in the decision so they asked him for his opinion because he could take a disinterested view of the situation.

The distinction between these two words is gradually dying out but many academics feel strongly that it should be retained.

Malapropisms

This odd word refers to words which sound vaguely similar and therefore get confused. They can have hilarious consequences - as many essay "howlers" demonstrate. (They are named after a character in a play who used these all the time).

It often happens when you use a word you have heard in a particular context but never seen written. You have actually mis-heard it - or, at least, mis-remembered it. For example **confines** and **confounds** sound very similar; **mitigate** and **militate** get confused for the same reason

 This is not permitted within the confounds of this society

 Social conditions mitigate against this happening

 When you are writing about unfamiliar subjects you have to use some unfamiliar words. Make sure you really understand them before you use them. And don't use unfamiliar words when you don't have to. Words used just to impress the reader never do. They either obscure the meaning or, at worst, sound ridiculous.

Ambiguous words

Many words can have more than one meaning and, if you are not careful which words you use, you can often say something you did not really mean.

 The people in the sample have been broken down by age and sex.

In this sentence **broken down** can mean two things. Either the people in the sample have been categorised according to their age and their sex, or the people themselveshave been destroyed by a combination of age and sex! If you are using the expression

intentionally - for humour, for example - there is no problem. It often happens, however, because you have not really thought about the words you have used.

It also happens when you use very colloquial expressions - the sort of thing you are likely to use in conversation rather than writing.

There are no absolute rules about how to avoid this kind of ambiguity but it will help if you make sure that you **devote one revision of your finished essay to checking your choice of words**.

Overcompression of meaning into too few words

A very common error made by students is trying to get too much meaning into too few words. This makes the meaning unclear and the reader has great difficulty deciphering what you are trying to say. It often happens when you try to express an idea in a phrase when it would be much easier - and clearer - if you used a whole sentence.

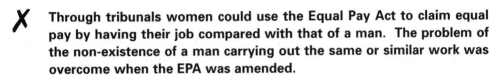

X **Through tribunals women could use the Equal Pay Act to claim equal pay by having their job compared with that of a man. The problem of the non-existence of a man carrying out the same or similar work was overcome when the EPA was amended.**

This would be much clearer if it were expanded

✓ **Through tribunals women could use the Equal Pay Act to claim equal pay by having their job compared with that of a man. There was a problem, however, when there was no man in the same workplace doing a comparable job. This problem was overcome when the EPA was amended.**

Sometimes, as in the paragraph in question 16, it is a whole paragraph that has been compressed into a single sentence. The sentence then reads like a list drawn from your notes - which it often is! The solution is to expand it.

✓ **If you are having difficulty explaining something clearly don't try to do it in as few words as possible just to get it out of the way! Break down the idea into clear units and use a sentence to express each one.**

Spelling

The spelling system of the English language causes everyone problems! But spelling is important if your work is to command serious attention. Bad spelling diverts the reader's attention from what you are saying - and it is very irritating. It is not conducive to putting any reader or marker in a positive frame of mind to consider your work.

For many difficult-to-spell words there are no rules and you just have to learn them. However, there are some rules and it is a good idea to learn what they are because it cuts down the number of words you have to learn by rote.

Double letters

Consonants (all the letters **except** a,e,i,o and u) cause the most problems in this respect. Why does **get** become **getting** whereas **meet** becomes **meeting**?

There are basic rules for this - though there are some exceptions.

Short words

If a short word has a short-sounding vowel sound (a,e,i,o,u) in the middle, then the final consonant is doubled if you add something that starts with another vowel to it

- **get**   **getting**
- **hot**   **hotter**

If the bit added to it begins with a consonant then no doubling takes place.

- **fit**   **fitment**

If a short word has a long-sounding vowel in the middle then you don't double the final consonant, whatever you add to it

- **meet**   **meeting**
- **pain**   **painful**

Longer words

These operate according to a different rule. What happens to the final consonant when you add an extra bit onto the word depends on which part of the word is emphasised when you say it.

- omit
- occur
- focus
- offer

All these words have two parts to them, but only one part of the word has the emphasis (stress). The problem is that this stress comes in different places. In **omit** and **occur** the second part of the word is stressed when you say it. In **focus** and **offer** the first part of the word has the stress.

● **If the second part has the emphasis - like omit and occur**

When you add to these words, and the addition starts with a vowel, you double the consonant at the end of the original word.

- omitted
- occurring
- inferred
- omitting

If the bit you add starts with a consonant, you do not double the original final consonant.

- commitment
- interment

● **If the first part of the word has the stress - like focus and offer**

When you add to these words, whatever the extra bit begins with, you do not double the original final consonant.

- focusing
- offered

- **The most important exception to this is words that end with a single - l.**

When you add to them and the bit you add begins with a vowel you do double the - l (except in US English!) whichever part of the word has the emphasis.

- travel
- model

- travelling
- modelled

-i and -ie

You probably already know the **-i before -e except after -c** rule. It works with most words

- receive
- achieve

- conceive
- relieve

- perceive
- retrieve

There are - as always - a few exceptions, but not many.

-ly endings

Words can be made to change their function by adding endings of different kinds. One very commonly used ending is -ly.

- common   commonly
- complete   completely
- simple   simply

These endings usually cause no problems. **The rule is that you add -ly to the original word, as in common+ly** and **frequent+ly.** This applies to most words - even those that end in -e, as in **complete+ly.**

The most obvious exceptions are those words that end in -e that **lose** the -e when the -ly is added - like **simply.** They are usually words where the -e is not there to alter the sound of the preceding vowel (the -e at the end of **complete** changes the sound of the -e in the middle of the word; the -e in **simple** does not change the sound of the -i in the middle).

-er or -or

- **Both -er and -or are used at the ends of words that describe people who do things and there is no rule for when to use which.**

    - actor, collector, doctor

    - reader, adviser, lecturer

- **The most frequent ending found on words for things that do something is - or**

    - generator, motor, distributor

The most frequently used exception is **computer**

-able and -ible

There are many complicated rules for deciding which of these two endings is the right one, but there are a few simple ones too. They do not work on all occasions but they do apply often enough to make it worthwhile your learning them

- **If the word they are being added to is a complete word in its own right, then the ending will probably be -able.**

    - advise   advisable
    - tax   taxable

    Note that the final -e of the original word gets omitted. This does not happen if the original words ends in -ce or -ge

    - pronounce   pronounceable
    - manage   manageable
    - change   changeable

- **If the word before the ending is not a complete word in its own right then the ending will probably be -ible**

    - horrible
    - edible
    - feasible

-sion and -tion

Which of these you use when forming a word is often determined by the ending of the word from which it is formed.

- **The ending -sion is often used for words formed from another word ending in**

-nd	expand	expansion
-de	provide	provision
-ss	discuss	discussion
-mit	omit	omission
-pel	compel	compulsion
-vert	revert	reversion

- **The ending -tion is often used for words formed from another word ending in**

-ct	act	action
-te	proliferate	proliferation
-pose	expose	exposition

-ant or -ent, -eous or -ious, -ceed,-cede or -sede

There are no generally applicable, easy rules for when you use these

there, their and they're

These are often used as if they were interchangeable! Make sure you know **now** which is which.

- **They're** is never appropriate in academic essays because it is an abbreviation of **they** and **are**. So for this purpose forget that form.

- **There** means **in that place**. It is also used in the expression **there is** (and all the other forms such as **there are, there were, there will be**)

- **Their** means **belonging to them**.

It really is that simple!

Some frequently-used words follow no rules at all.

You must simply learn them. Choose the ones **you** use most frequently **first**.

- abbreviated
- character
- development
- exaggerated
- negative
- occasionally
- omission
- parallel
- relative
- separate
- successful

Spelling causes everyone problems at some time But remember – bad spelling looks illiterate even when the writing is otherwise very fluent. Spell-checks on word processors help, but they do not completely solve the problem. They are not fool-proof because if you use the wrong spelling for the word with that meaning in that context, but the word you have written is a word in its own right, the spell-check will not be able to identify the error. There is, therefore, no substitute for learning frequently-used words and looking up others in the dictionary

Punctuation of individual words

Apostrophes

These are frequently misused. The **basic** rules for their use are very simple. There are two main reasons for using them.

To mark abbreviations

An apostrophe is used to show that letters are missing. Some very pedantic writers will, for example, use the apostrophe at the beginning of the word **'phone** to show that **tele-** has been omitted. This is unnecessary but it illustrates the point. The most common places to use them in writing are in situations such as

- **We're going**
- **You've been there**
- **It's late**

Once again examples from casual speech have been used because that is where this feature occurs most often. Therefore, if you are writing a novel you need to use them. **You should, however, never need them in essays or reports because these forms are informal and therefore not appropriate in formal writing.** (I've used them in this book - deliberately - because it's meant to be user-friendly rather than formal!) In essays you need to use the full form each time.

- **We are going**
- **You have been there**
- **It is late**

The only situation where it's has an apostrophe is when it means it is. So in essays you should always write its (just as you write his not hi's)

To mark ownership or possession

●   **-'s or -s' are used to mark ownership or possession**

    ■   **The author's book**
    ■   **The company's accounts**

●   The rule here is that the apostrophe occurs in the word naming the owner and it comes after the actual word that names the owner

    The **book** belongs to the **author**. The word naming the owner is **author** so –'s is added to the word **author**.

    ■   **the author's book**

    The **accounts** belong to the **company** so -'s is added to **company**. (There is only one company in this case).

    ■   **the company's accounts**

●   When the owner is plural (when there is more than one) the rule is slightly different - but only slightly.

    ■   **The authors' books**
    ■   **The companies' accounts**

This time there are more than one author, more than one company. The books belong to the **authors**. The accounts belong to the **companies**.

The rule for showing ownership would suggest that you write

- **The authors's book**
- **The companies's accounts**

But because **authors** and **companies** already have an **-s** at the end, the second one is not necessary so it is deleted.

● The "old" rule of adding -s' if the word is plural does not always work because some words do not have an **-s** in the plural form - **children,** for example.

■ **The Children's Charter**

The Charter "belongs" to the **children**. So you add -'s to **children**. The word **children** is plural, but it doesn't use an **-s** to mark this so it needs the **-s** as well as the apostrophe.

● Some words that are **not** plural end in **-s**. Here the rule is still add -'s. The difference is that the **-s** remains even though you've already got one. You end up with two, as in **Burns's poetry**.

● Whether the other word in the group - the word that does not name the owner - is singular or plural, doesn't matter. It is only the word naming the owner that matters.

Words that are simply plural never need apostrophes

■ **Most individuals use aggressive behaviour at some time.**

Individuals simply means that more than one individual is being referred to. Nobody owns anything, so no apostrophe is needed.

Inverted commas

(Their use in bibliographies is dealt with in **Section 6** in the subsection dealing with bibliographies).

To mark quotations

If you are quoting anything - from a book, a film, what someone said - you need to enclose the quoted words in inverted commas. This applies to single words and phrases as well as whole sentences.

- **The water is described as "ghostly" and "corpse-like".**
- **Words of violence such as "break", "bruise", "blow" and " bind" occur frequently in this verse.**

(There is a lot more about how to use quotations in **Section 6**).

To alter the meaning of a word

Many words in English have various shades of meaning. If you want to indicate to the reader that the word or phrase you are using is to be read and understood in an unusual way you enclose the word or phrase in inverted commas.

- **<u>Animal Farm</u> by George Orwell is a "fairy story".**
- **The Charter "belongs" to the children.**

The first of these suggests that the book is not literally a book about fairies, but that it is to be interpreted by the readers in the much the same way as they interpret fairy stories.

The second suggests that the Charter does not belong to the children in the literal sense but that it is related to them and **belongs** should be interpreted as meaning this.

SECTION 7

SAMPLE ESSAYS

History

Question

Why did the Conservative Party dominate the political scene in the 1930's?

Structure

Introduction - essay in two main sections

Introduction to why the Conservatives won the 1931 election.

Reasons why former Liberals switched allegiance to the Conservatives.

Reasons why the Liberals did not switch to Labour.

The question posed can be conveniently dealt with in two parts; firstly the reasons for the attainment of ascendancy; and secondly the reasons for the retention of that ascendancy.

Britain between 1929 and 1931 had a minority Labour government led by Ramsay MacDonald. The fact that the National Government formed in 1931 came into being as a result of an election where the Conservatives won 474 out of the 556 National Government seats, has its roots in the preceding two decades.

Before the Great War the Conservatives' main rivals had been the Liberal party. Committed to non-intervention and free trade the Liberals rapidly showed that they were unsuited to govern in war-time. Asquith was perceived as weak and ineffective. This led to a split in the Liberal party in 1916 with Lloyd George's faction forming a coalition with the Conservatives in the election of 1918 where the Conservatives won 338 of the coalition's 484 seats. Many Liberal voters thus lost confidence in the party and switched their allegiance to the Conservatives.

These Liberal voters did not switch to Labour for a number of reasons. Firstly they had been alienated by the fact that Labour had withdrawn from an earlier pact with the Liberals and, secondly, it had, by the 1930's, come to be dominated by the trade unions. and had assumed the appearance, if not the reality, of being the party of left wing politics. This impression was reinforced by the fact that it had also split with the Fabian Society and was later to split with the Independent Labour Party (in 1932). By 1931 Labour party organisation was also weak. There was a decline in the number of full time election agents, and the unemployment that had been growing since 1927 had led to a drop in funds. In some areas constituency organisations had ceased to exist. In others reliance was placed on trade union organisers. As a consequence they lacked the continuity of the Conservative organisations between elections. The Liberal party organisation by this stage was also in disarray and by the time of the 1931 election was unable to contest as many seats. In 1929 it had put up 512 candidates. In 1931 it put up only 160. In about 375 constituencies Liberal voters who wanted to support the National Government candidate found that they had to vote Conservative.

The Conservatives by contrast had a more efficient party organisation which had its roots in the Victorian period. The Conservatives had a system for training and examining party agents. They took steps to improve this. In the period between 1924 and 1937 they trained 352 election agents and 99 women organisers. They particularly provided (as they had done in the Victorian era) a role for women in the party organisation, and by 1929 women represented 52.7% of the electorate. Studies of the elections between 1918 and 1931 show a tendency for women to vote Conservative. The result was that in 1931 the Liberal vote tumbled from 5.3 million to 2.3 million. The Conservative vote rose from 8.6 million to 11.9 million.

Conservative success because of the efficiency of the party organisation.

The Conservative party was also wealthier partly due to its closer association with the wealthier interests, but partly also due to the fact that they placed great emphasis upon fund raising, especially on raising large numbers of small subscriptions. This was possible because the party appealed to people across the social spectrum. Since Victorian times the Conservative party has always been the party of patriotism. Such notions still had a broad popular appeal even amongst the working classes. The high Conservative content of the post 1931 government is thus explicable in terms of the broad appeal to all classes of the call for national unity in the face of the much publicised national crisis in the newspapers of 1930-31.

Conservative success because of the broad appeal.

Other external factors also helped the Conservatives to gain such a large percentage of seats in the 1931 election. Firstly, the granting of Irish independence in 1922 served to reduce the Conservative's opposition. The Irish had been allies of the Liberals in the period prior to the Great War. After 1922, however, the separation of the Republic left Ulster with 12 Westminster MP's, not more than 2 of whom were ever other than Unionist. A block of opposition had thus been removed and a small level of support had been gained.

External factors affecting Conservative popularity in Ireland

Redistribution of seats in 1918 also supported the Conservatives as a result of the modifications made to constituencies. University representation was increased from 9 to 15 (something of a surprise to the Conservatives: they had expected to lose these completely). Also the rules for constituency size seem to have been applied with some latitude. While certain Liberal

Redistribution of seats was another important external factor

counties which were sparsely populated became amalgamated others seemed to have been given the benefit of the doubt where their population did not fall too far below the statutory limit. A Conservative source estimated that some 17 seats had been saved in this way.

The first past the post electoral system also worked to the Conservatives' advantage in the 1930's. In 1929 Labour had won, partly because they had faced a greater number of three cornered contests. In 1929 there were 447 such contents whereas in 1931 there were only 99. A three cornered contest significantly increased the chances of winning by a modest majority with a comparatively smaller share of the vote. With Liberal votes defecting to the conservatives and the increased number of seats where no Liberal stood in 1931, Conservative domination was assured within the National Government.

The electoral system was another important external factor

Hence the Conservatives achieved ascendancy -and they proceeded to retain it.

Introduction to why the Conservatives continued in power.

One of the major factors was their handling of the economy. It had been a problem for a long time previously.The second Labour Government had assumed power at a time of serious financial crisis. Britain was still on the gold standard. The commitment to the old staple industries which were uncompetitive led to a decline in exports and a deficit in the balance of payments. The commitment to unemployment insurance was also helping to bankrupt the Government since unemployment levels were high. There was, therefore, a pressing need to cut Government spending, to produce a balanced budget and above all to restore confidence in the British economy, not just at home but also abroad. However, as the financial crisis deepened the Labour Cabinet split on the question of whether unemployment insurance should be reduced. Faced with such indecision, the economic policy became one of drift. The situation became so serious that the prime minister reached the conclusion that the Gordian knot must be cut. The National Government was thus born with Ramsay MacDonald at its head and a General Election followed three months later. Because the new National Government enjoyed massive popular support it confidently produced new economic policies. The old notions of free trade were abandoned, Britain came off the gold standard and protection measures were introduced. Coming off gold produced an almost immediate improvement in trade. It had the incidental effect of protecting upper working class and middle class savings which no doubt assisted in promoting notions of recovery in the popular consciousness.

Their handling of the economy was good.

The National Government's decision to abandon free trade also had the effect of ensuring that the Liberal Party split remained permanent. Some Liberals were fierce advocates of free trade while those who supported the National Government endorsed the protectionist policy. The Liberal Party therefore, sustained more lasting damage in the election of 1931 than did the Labour Party which quickly adjusted to the idea that protectionism should be taken for granted.

However the Labour Party was plagued by a number of other problems. Firstly, with the departure of MacDonald and other national Labour candidates to the National Government there was a leadership vacuum both before the 1931 election and after. In the recriminations and accusations of treachery which followed the events of August, 1931 a crisis of confidence can be detected particularly about the direction which Labour politics should take. A debate commenced as to whether a more radical political stance should be adopted. The moderates, however, ultimately won and their national plan was seen as a corrective adjustment to capitalism rather than an alternative to it. Thus specifically Labour policies did not gain popular support.

In 1935 the economic recovery also effectively robbed the Labour Party of a central line of attack. One million houses had been built since 1931. The 1935 budget restored 1931 cuts in salaries and unemployment insurance rates and also restored reliefs from income tax. Extra funds were provided for road building to help the unemployed. Labour clearly were hard put to complain about such measures. National Government was perceived to have been beneficial: it offered something for everyone. Much of the Labour Party's thunder had thus been stolen. Labour's chances were also not helped by the Communist Party which published its manifesto on the same day as Labour. The Communists stated that they had withdrawn all candidates except two to ensure the return of a Labour Government. It was thus easy for the National Government's supporters to point to a perceived connection between the Labour Party and the Stalinist Russia and dissuade the electorate from voting for them.

Winning the 1935 election, therefore, was due to the credibility of the National Government in the eyes of the erstwhile Labour and Liberal voters. Neville Chamberlain assumed control of the Conservative Party in 1937 and the party's dominance remained until the outbreak of the Second World War. Later Stanley Baldwin's skilful leadership was a vital factor in securing continued Conservative domination. His slightly left of centre policies, his measured reticence on the question of re-armament when public opinion was still strongly pacifist, and his emasculation of the right wing of his party matched the mood of the times. His policies helped to make the difference between National Government and Labour less pronounced. His skilful use of the media helped him to radiate a wholesome almost nonpolitical appeal which was the envy of his rivals. His politics were centrist, liberal and conciliatory.

Conservatism's continued success after the election of 1931, *Conclusion* therefore, was based on its broad appeal. Most voters wanted a government which seemed non-controversial and which would achieve a moderate degree of success. The achievement of such a record was endorsed by an electorate which was all too mindful of the crises in the period leading up to 1931. With hindsight, however,it seems that its success was a tribute to the ability of the party to adapt - to adapt to the changing electorate in the post 1918 era, to the changing economy, and to the changing international situation. It would require the dislocation of the Second World War before Labour would again defeat them.

Bibliography

Branson, N. & Heineman, M., (1973) *Britain in the 1930's*, Panther, St Albans

Eatwell, R. & Wright, A., (1978) Labour and the Lessons of 1931, *History 63*

Lindsay, T. F. & Harrington, M., Ramsden, J., (1974) *The Conservative Party 1918-79*, Macmillan London

Stevenson, J. & Cook C., (1977) *The Slump : Society and Politics during the Depression*, Cape, London

Pugh, M., (1982) *The Making of Modern British Politics 1867-1939*, Blackwell, Oxford

Williamson, P., (1992) *National Crisis and National Government*, Cambridge UP, Cambridge

Wilson, T., (1966) *The Downfall of the Liberal Party*, Collins, London

Comment

This essay illustrates very well how to break down the subject being discussed into different topic areas - how to **analyse** the subject.

The introduction suggests that the essay is divided into only two main sections. But the writer has actually divided each of these into a number of different sub-sections. (Section "headings" have been added in the margin to show where each of these sub-sections begins and what it is about). The writer has indicated this in the introductory sentence of each sub-section.

There is only one important thing wrong with the structure of this essay. The section dealing with the period after the 1931 election is rather hurried, and much less well discussed than the reasons why the Conservatives did so well in the election itself. Many of the points need further justification and proof. They need to be further "developed".

Some history lecturers would also be concerned about the lack of references within the text - especially in relation to facts where controversial comments are being made. It is important to ask the views of the person for whom you are writing.

The mark for this essay was B+

Applied Social Science

Question

The decline of the private rented sector has been one of the most consistent features of the twentieth century. Explain the trend and discuss the prospects for attempts to resurrect this sector.

Structure and Comment

One of the most obvious changes in British housing in the twentieth century has been the decline of the private rented sector. Before the First World War private landlords controlled the majority of rented accommodation in both Scotland and Britain. From 1914 to the present day both their physical stock and their share of the rental market have been in continual decline. This has been particularly sharp since 1945. The decline has been attributed to rent controls,the increase in better investment opportunities elsewhere and the growth of owner occupation and council renting. In recent times there have been a number of attempts to resurrect this sector.

Brief introduction. Nevertheless gives outline of content and order of what is to be discussed later. (Doesn't indicate success of attempts to resurrect sector. This is for conclusion).

In the late nineteenth and early twentieth centuries the housing stock was overwhelmingly in the hands of private landlords. This sector accounted for 7.1m dwellings or 90% of the total housing stock in England and Wales in 1914. At the same time owner occupation accounted for no more than 10% and council renting around 1% of the housing stock in Britain (Daunton, 1987). By 1975, however, the number of private rented sector dwellings had fallen to 2.9m or 16% of the stock, a net loss of 4.2m (DOE, 1977). More recently, the size of the sector has fallen further to 7.7% of the stock in England and Wales (Malpass and Murie,1990) and 5.9% of the stock in Scotland. (SDD, 1988)

Details decline. (Note frequent references because facts taken from other writers).

The causes of the decline are well documented. (Kemp,1980: Gibb, 1990) The imposition of legislation, to control rent and give security of tenure has been seen as the main cause. They were first introduced to prevent private sector landlords from taking advantage of a housing shortage that developed during the First

Suggests causes of decline (next three paragraphs). Each one deals with different cause.

World War in areas of munitions production. Some landlords exploited the situation by raising rents and justified their actions by claiming that they were off-setting higher rates of interest on borrowed capital. This created resentment amongst working class tenants and a wave of rent strikes took place throughout the country. This forced the State, which until then had showed no signs of intervening, to pass emergency legislation at the end of 1915 to control rent levels. The Increase in Rent and Mortgage Interest (War Restrictions) Act (1915) fixed most rents at the level of August 1914. The effect of this was to reduce the flow of investment into housing because it reduced a landlord's rate of return on capital. No private landlord would continue investing in an unprofitable market. After the war, and for the next twenty years or so, rent controls were removed in stages and then, just as the economics of private renting were becoming more attractive to landlords again, the Second World War broke out and rent controls were re-introduced. The experience of twenty years previously was then repeated.

The use of legislation to control the level of rents in this way had another serious effect on the private rented sector. Even before 1914 concern was being expressed at the flight of capital from the housing market but as rent controls reduced landlords' profits still further they looked around for better investment opportunities. As a result there was a flow of capital out of Britain, overseas. After 1914 it became even more serious as alternative investments offered a better combination of risk and return. *More causes of decline*

At the same time other forms of housing provision became more attractive to tenants. First of all owner occupation became a viable and more attractive option for households - including those on moderate incomes - for a number of reasons (Ball,1983). There had, first of all, been a real growth in incomes, and the first Building Societies had become really established. Furthermore - particularly in the inter-war period - the massive development of subsidised public sector housing, built to a standard at least as good as that found in the majority of private sector dwellings, made housing available to those who could not buy. The combined result of these factors was the massive decline in the demand for private rented housing detailed earlier. *More causes of decline*

Since 1979 there have been attempts to revitalise the private rented sector. The two most important of these were the Housing Acts of 1980 and 1988. The Housing Act (1980) contained a package of measures aimed at making rented housing an attractive investment for potential landlords, especially in high demand areas. In the first place the Fair Rents system was reformed. A Rent Officer had previously been able to set a rent if one could not be agreed between landlord and tenant. Once registered, this rent level was binding for three years.The 1980 *Describes attempts to resurrect sector by Housing legislation. Judges effectiveness. (Needs to justify judgement).*

Act reduced the period to two years. It also transferred older (pre-1965) controlled rents to this system. This, as intended, had the effect of raising these older rents. The two Acts also created two new forms of private tenancy. Shorthold tenancies in England and Wales (1980), and short assured tenancies in Scotland (1988) gave the landlord a guarantee of vacant possession after a fixed period of renting (1 -5 years). Later the conditions of the shorthold tenancy were changed to allow market rents (rather than fair rents) to be set for new tenancy agreements. A survey later found that 14% of all new lettings were shorthold (Todd 1986). Assured tenancies were also introduced (in the 1980 Act in England and Wales and in 1988 in Scotland). They allowed market rents to be charged on lets in new developments and were aimed at creating an increased supply of new lets.This type of tenancy has since been extended to cover lets other than those in new build developments. However, all these measures to revive the private rented sector had little impact.

The Housing Act (1988) was accompanied by two related measures also designed to make private renting more attractive to investors.The Business Expansion Scheme (BES) was one of them. It offered tax free incentives up to £40,00 to investors prepared to commit money for five years. These incentives meant the subsequent sales of shares in housing developments were not subject to Capital Gains tax. The success of this was limited, however, by the fact that a rate of return of around 9% gross was needed and this was difficult to achieve in the rented housing sector unless the investment was in housing at the upper end of the market.

Describes attempts to resurrect sector by other legislation. Judges effectiveness. (Justification better. Facts need references).

The second measure - in Scotland - had more effect. Scottish Homes was given powers to provide finance in different ways - in the form of grants for example - to private landlords to reduce the supply price of rented provision. Scottish Homes is a National Housing Agency, created on 1 April 1989 from a merger between Scottish Special Housing Association and the Housing Corporation in Scotland. It aims "to make sure the quality of housing and variety of housing options available in Scotland are substantially improved." *(Scottish Homes Annual Review*, 1992-3). One of the objectives designed to support the achievement of this aim is to promote" the development of a more diverse rented sector". If it is to do this, it must "harness the considerable resources of all housing providers, including those of the private rented sector". In this task the existing partnerships between Scottish Homes, financial institutions and private landlords and developers have already helped towards realising that vision of diversity. During 1992-3 grants amounting to £49m were approved by Scottish Homes to fund new developments throughout Scotland which provided 309 new or improved houses for private rental (*Scottish Homes Annual*

Describes only "successful" measure. Judgement controversial (so needs much more justification).

Review 1992-3). The fact that they intend to continue to do this was suggested as recently as December 1993, when they called for more private investments in housing projects (*The Scotsman* 3 December 1993).

It is clear then that the private rented sector has suffered a dramatic decline since the beginning of the century. For various reasons the efforts to revive it in the form of legislation in the 1980s had only limited success. In Scotland the legislation that created Scottish Homes in 1988 has had some, more positive impact on the private rented sector. However, attempts to capitalise on these will only be successful when innovative and practical initiatives to attract new investment can be devised.

Bibliography

Ball, M., (1983) *Housing Policy & Economic Power,* Methuen, London

Best, R., (ed), (1991), *A New Century in Social Housing,* Leicester University Press

DOE, (1977), *Housing Policy : Technical Volume, Part iii*

Daunton, M. J., (1987), "The Collapse of the Old Order" in *A Property Owning Democracy,* Faber & Faber

Gibb, K., (1990), *The Problem of Private Renting,* Centre for Housing Research Discussion Paper, Glasgow

Kemp, P., (1988), *The Future of Private Renting,* University of Salford

Malpass, P. and Murie, A., (1990), *Housing Policy and Practice,* MacMillan (3rd ed)

Scotsman Publications, (1993), "Housing Agency in Private Cash Call" in *The Scotsman* on 3 December 1993

Todd, J., (1986), *Recent Private Lettings 1982-1984,* HMSO, London

Scottish Homes, *Annual Review and Summary Financial Statement, 1992/1993*

SDD, (1988), *Housing Act (Scotland)*

Comment

For a first essay, written by a new student in Housing Policy and Practice this is perfectly acceptable. The recommended mark was 70%.

It is a well structured and coherent account, especially in its description of the decline in the amount of private rented housing. It is very easy to go into far too much detail and fail to highlight the really significant developments in writing this kind of account. This then overbalances the essay in that it gives too much weight to the description of the background and not enough to a discussion of the issues. This essay gives the background succinctly and still includes the main points.

Other issues that could have been usefully included are the decline in the public image of private renting and the subsequent change in the social and economic profile of private rented sector tenants; the lessons that can be learned from the failure of the Business Expansion Scheme; and the implications of all this in general for public subsidy in housing. Discussion of the effectiveness of the legislation could be strengthened by going into more detail about what effect in had - or didn't have - and the reasons for it. (This kind of justification is especially necessary when making judgements that many people would disagree with.)

The writer of this essay needs to remember that all points of arguments need justifying by the use of evidence and all evidence needs referencing.

The style of writing is clear and free from jargon. The technical vocabulary - **new build, new lets, private rented sector** - is all quite comprehensible to any thoughtful reader and is necessary to refer to situations quickly and accurately.

Sociology

Question

What part did the development of mechanical means of contraception play in the late nineteenth century decline in fertility?

Structure and Comment

In the late nineteenth century there was a marked decline in the birth rate. This coincided with mechanical means of contraception becoming widely available for the first time. It is tempting, therefore , to see this as the main cause of the decline in fertility but it is important to question whether this was the only - or even the main -cause.

Clear definition of the problem and statement of the two main elements of the question to be dealt with.

To begin with, contraception was practised long before the decline in fertility began. Three types of contraception - abortion, coitus interruptus and abstinence - have existed for hundreds of years. Although they were available, however, they were not effective as mass means of birth control. Abortion was illegal in Britain until quite recently so we do not have reliable figures on exactly how widely practised it was but its dangers and illegality obviously limited its general use as a means of birth control. Coitus interruptus and abstinence also have obvious disadvantages which limited their effectiveness too. Therefore the introduction of mechanical means of contraception provided women especially with a safe and reliable means of birth control for the first time.

Brief description (two paragraphs) of historical background and contraceptive methods available at time in question. (All the facts quoted need references).

One such innovation was the contraceptive douche which was invented in the 1830s by an American physicist called Charles Knowlton. He also produced The Fruits of Philosophy which was the first good pamphlet on contraceptive techniques, published in the USA. Another breakthrough was the Dutch Cap which was described in 1838 by a German physician, Dr. Friedrich Adolphe Wilde. The contraceptive sponge, publicised by Francis Place, was also available at the time of the decline in the birth rate.

However, it is not likely that these devices had any great effect on the conception rate because they were not widely used partly because of the cost. Condoms too had limited impact for similar

Discussion of reasons why not responsible

reasons. Skin condoms had been available since the eighteenth century but they were not widely used because the cost was too high. Working class people could not afford them. In 1843 when the Goodyear Rubber Company vulcanized rubber in the USA and Hancock did the same in Britain it became possible to mass produce them and they therefore became widely available by the 1880s. However, even then the cost was between five and ten shillings when the weekly wage was only around twenty five shillings. Other mechanical means of contraception were similarly expensive so it seems unlikely that any of them were used by the working class population. It does not seem possible then, that they had much effect on the fertility decline in its early stages.

Another reason why mechanical means of contraception were not widely used is that they had a very poor public image. This is conveniently illustrated by what happened in the case of condoms. They were associated with male promiscuity and were used mainly to prevent men catching venereal disease from prostitutes. Their prime purpose, therefore, was not seen as being for protection from unwanted pregnancies and their public image discouraged their general use. Other mechanical means of birth control suffered the same reputation by association. In addition to this birth control itself was seen by some as an immoral practice, and was thought to be a sin against the Holy Ghost. Even information about methods of contraception, therefore, was though of as being filthy and obscene so there was very little of it in circulation.

All this changed, however, in 1877 when Charles Bradlaugh and Annie Besant decided to re-issue Charles Knowlton's pamphlet on birth control *The Fruits of Philosophy*. Its publication in Britain was illegal so Charles Bradlaugh and Annie Besant were put on trial. Ironically this did more to widen public awareness of birth control than earlier efforts to do so directly. Details of the trial were published very fully in the national press and local papers. This was the first time that the subject had been discussed so publicly and openly. The publicity caused by the trial also caused the sales of *The Fruits of Philosophy* to rise considerably. Therefore many women, especially working class women, learned of the availability of contraception for the first time. This undoubtedly had an effect on the birth rate.

Important though all this was, however, it cannot have been the only factor. For one thing, the decline in the birth rate began before 1877 which would suggest that the availability of the mechanical means of contraception was not the only cause. Another possible reason is related to the economics of the period. The late nineteenth century was a time of great economic change. It was a time of remarkably growth and middle class and working class people had more money than ever before.

for birth-rate decline. Change in direction of argument clearly signalled by first sentence. Two main reasons in two separate paragraphs. (Facts, figures needed to prove statements).

Explanation of how knowledge of contraception became more widespread. (Facts need referencing).

Change of direction in argument signalled well. Three alternative reasons for decline detailed, but grouped together because all economic

165

Expectations about standards of living therefore changed and both middle and working classes wanted to buy goods and services in order to fulfil these expectations. A large family would prevent them from doing this. An additional pressure was the fact that education for children had been made compulsory and it cost money. Also a decline in child employment meant that children no longer contributed to the family's finances. All these factors. therefore, provided people with the motive for wanting to limit family size.

Another possible cause of the decline in fertility is connected with industrialisation and a decline in infant mortality. The growth of the availability of factory work led to a decline in the fertility rate first of all because it reduced the number of illegitimate births. This was because working class women no longer had to go into domestic service where they were sexually vulnerable. Instead they could live at home and work in the local factory. However, this was not the major influence that factory work had on the birth rate. The local availability of work for working class women, linked with a desire for a higher standard of living meant that working class women were choosing to work rather than have a large family. At the same time the need to have a large family was being reduced by falling levels of infant mortality. When infant mortality is high it is difficult for the individual to exercise any choice over family size since the well-being of the family unit and the community as a whole depends on a high fertility rate. However, when mortality rates fell it was possible to exercise a conscious control over family size. So when improvements in health care and sanitation came about and infant mortality declined it became possible, as well as desirable to limit family size.

It is obvious, therefore, that economic change and increasing prosperity for individuals contributed to the late nineteenth century decline infertility. However, the fact that the mechanical means of contraception became available at this time undoubtedly played its part since the motives for limiting family size and the means by which it could be done occurred simultaneously. As awareness and understanding grew fertility declined even further. The availability of mechanical meant of contraception may not, therefore,have been the cause of this decline but it was almost certainly the means by which it was accomplished.

reasons. (Proof needed to justify arguments).

Conclusion relating two strands of argument to each other. Satisfactorily neat.

Conclusion

Bibliography

Hawthorn, G., (1970) *The Sociology of Fertility*, Princeton University Press

Banks, J A., Banks, O., (1954) *The Bradlaugh/Besant Trial and the English Newspapers,* Population Studies

Tranter, N L, (1985) *Population and Society 1750-1940,* London, Longman

Carlsson, G., (1967) *Innovation or Adjustment Process,* Population Studies

Teitelbaum, M S., (1984) *The British Fertility Decline,* Princeton University Press

Comment

This is a well balanced essay that weighs the impact of contraception against other possible factors. The writer has read the implications of the question as well as its more explicit requirements. **What part did X play** usually suggests that other factors probably played a part as well.

The writer has not fallen into the trap of writing about the subject in a purely chronological way. The structure of the argument is based on a thoughtful and logical approach to the question -

- a decline in fertility happened;
- it coincided with the development of contraception
- did it cause the decline?
- what else could have caused it?
- was there any relationship between these causes and the availability of contraception?

This kind of thought process shows "good critical abilities" and gives the essay a structure that is clear and logical.

The argument is seriously flawed, however, by the lack of evidence for the points made. They are simply asserted without being proved in any way. Statistics, research findings reported in other writers' work, examples and quotations providing corroborative evidence of attitudes at the time - all suitably referenced - would all help to make the argument more convincing.

The recommended grade was B.

English

Question

Comment on the narrative style of the following passage, relating your analysis where possible to the methods and concerns of the story as a whole: Flannery O'Connor: *Revelation* : from p 213 `Mrs Turpin didn't catch every word ...' to p 214 `And dirtier than a hog, she added to herself.'

O'Connor's `Revelation' centres on a climactic day's experience for its protagonist, Mrs Turpin. Though not split up formally, the narrative falls into two parts, the first recounting the conversation between patients in a doctor's waiting room, where Mrs Turpin is attacked physically and verbally by the `ugly girl' who has been observing her with increasing malevolence throughout. After this we follow Mrs Turpin's return to her farmstead, where she broods on the meaning of the attack; as evening falls she sees a vision of souls making their way to paradise. Paradoxically this seems both to confirm and contradict her notions of herself as a virtuous and generous Christian person, whose material circumstances offer proof that she is particularly blessed by Christ. The story's setting is obviously the American South; the characters' prejudices about race and class, as well as religion, are at the centre of it moral structure.

The chosen passage occurs towards the middle of the first part of the story, and provides an example of the narrative method employed by O'Connor to characterise Mrs Turpin. Apart from a few scene-setting comments on her appearance (her `looming' largeness in the small waiting room, and her `bright black eyes' which `sized up the seating situation') we see the doctor's waiting room from Mrs Turpin's point of view: she is used by O'Connor as a `centre of consciousness'.

Mrs Turpin's thoughts are sparked off by a song on the radio about helping others. She regards herself as a `someone who never spared herself when she found somebody in need' (p 213). O'Connor offers an episode later in the story which is seen to support Mrs Turpin's generous assessment of herself. She talks to the black farm-workers in her employment, to whom she is giving water to drink at the end of their working day. The blacks appear to subscribe to her view of herself (`you the sweetest lady I know', p220) but we are left not really able to determine the real state of their mutual relations. Mrs Turpin treats them fairly enough, though like children. Strangely she seems to want to confide in them, but is irritated by their inscrutable flattery. Interestingly, she seems to require their moral support more than they require her water. Hence, the impression made upon the reader by Mrs Turpin is far more complex and ambiguous than her own generous self-assessment would at first suggest. Even at this early point in the story, what we already know of her leads us to doubt her complacent self-view. We have

168

already seen how she divides the people she meets according to her prejudices: are they 'white or black, trash or decent'? None of her harsh thoughts about her companions in the waiting room suggests much capacity for tolerance, sympathy or kindness. She is always qualifying her public comments with private, cruel observations. Several instances of this occur in the passage - her response to the 'pleasant lady's' explanation of her daughter's education, for example:

'way up north,' Mrs Turpin murmured and thought, well, it hasn't done much for her manners (p214).

In fact, in the first part of the story it is this discrepancy between Mrs Turpin's projection of herself and her private, mean-minded vision of people that commands the reader's attention. Because hers is the point of view from which the story is told we are forced to experience things though her judgement of them. The reader therefore feels discomfort as being forced to identify with her morally questionable attitudes. This discomfort is reinforced when the passage reverts to Mrs Turpin's categorisation of society according to colour, appearance and decency. She also imagines herself bargaining with Jesus as to what kind of person she would rather be. Here a new self-classification emerges: 'Make me a <u>good</u> woman and it don't matter what else, how fat or ugly or how poor' (p213). Her joy at what she sees as Jesus's generosity is disturbingly self-satisfied:

He had not made her a nigger or white-trash or ugly! He had made her herself and given her a little of everything. Jesus, thank you! she said.

O'Connor chooses at this point to remind us that Mrs Turpin is 'very large' (p 205), in a way that undercuts her present beatific self-assessment: 'Whenever she counted her blessings she felt as buoyant as if she weighed one hundred and twenty-five pounds instead of one hundred and eighty' (p 213).

However our reactions to her at this point are not ones of simple dislike or disapproval I feel there is something innocent as well as nasty in Mrs Turpin's complacency: she is indeed grateful and almost, for a moment, humble in her gratitude. It is at exactly such a moment, when she suffers 'a terrible pang of joy' (p 215) and cries out loud her gratitude to Jesus for her husband Claud (in whom we have been shown little to admire), that the girl attacks her. This all creates an ambiguity in the reader's reactions to Mrs Turpin. This same response is evoked by her thoughts about the 'white-trash woman', whom she judges as 'too lazy to light the fire'. We feel a tendency to disapprove, yet O'Connor makes that woman too a focus of the reader's dislike, chiefly for her animadversions about the 'niggers' whom she despises. She too seems intent on categorising society in terms of what she wouldn't do (keep hogs, for example); in this she ironically provides more of a parallel than a contrast to Mrs Turpin, in spite of what that lady thinks. The comment on her child, who was naturally 'mean', but 'took sick and turned good' (by which she means his current state of listless indifference) offers a curious counterpoint to Mrs Turpin's inner debates on the nature of 'goodness'.

However, it is still impossible to sympathise with Mrs Turpin's final statement of her attitude to the 'white-trash woman', which combines an apparently impartial out-loud comment on the potential decency of blacks (in fact a scarcely veiled insult) with an example of class bigotry of her own, expressed in the familiar language of intolerance:

If I was going to send anyone back to Africa, Mrs Turpin thought, it would be your kind woman. 'Yes, indeed', she said aloud, but looking up at the ceiling, 'it's a heap of things worse than a nigger'. And dirtier than a hog, she added to herself.

The other strand in this part of the story that attracts attention and seems significant is the oddity of the 'pleasant lady's' daughter, categorised by Mrs Turpin as 'the ugly girl'. Though we may sympathise with the girl's mounting anger at the small-minded bigotry of those around her, her focus on Mrs Turpin (not on Claud or the white-trash woman, for example, who both openly declare their racial prejudice) does seem peculiar:

> **All at once the ugly girl turned her lips inside out again. Her eyes were fixed like two drills on Mrs Turpin. This time there was no mistaking there was something urgent behind them.**

> **Girl, Mrs Turpin exclaimed silently, I haven't done a thing to you!**

O'Connor does not give us enough insight into the girl's violent anger to allow us to sympathise with her, though the way in which her mother irritatingly speaks for her in this passage, (rattling on about her studies at Wellesley), and the ensuing tirade about ingratitude, directed as it is against her daughter, offer grounds for compassion. Her name, Mary Grace, is clearly ironical and seems significant. Mrs Turpin interprets what the girl says about her being a 'wart hog from hell', as coming from God. It is as if the girl (like the reader, like God presumably) sees into Mrs Turpin's thoughts and loathes her complacency, prejudice and lack of charity.

Nothing that happens in the dirty, small waiting room - surely a metaphor for the sickness and original sin of humanity - prepares the reader for the final part of the story. They are, nevertheless, related to each other by the ugly girl. The climax of the story is the sunset vision of the 'vast horde of souls ... rumbling toward heaven' (p 224). Those categories of people in the waiting room to whom she feels morally superior seem to enter heaven with more ease and less pain than her own class:

> **There were whole companies of white-trash, clean for the first time in their lives, and bands of black niggers in white robes, and battalions of freaks and lunatics shouting and clapping and leaping like frogs.**

This last category would seem to include the 'ugly girl', bearer of the dreadful message, who is branded a lunatic by the 'white-trash woman'. In the vision Mrs Turpin and her sort do enter heaven, but only after their 'virtues' are 'burned away' in purgatorial fire. Such 'virtues' are demonstrated in the chosen passage: her complacent belief in her own goodness, her decency, her good 'disposition' and sense of respectability. O'Connor seems to be telling us through this final vision that Mrs Turpin is finally to be redeemed, but in spite of, not because of, her 'goodness'. That discomfort and moral awkwardness which the reader feels, seeing the world through Mrs Turpin's eyes, and the difficulties of her muddled perception of her goodness is finally resolved in this final, paradoxical 'abysmal life-giving vision'. Judgement and nature of goodness are the story's themes. The girl's insult in the passage foreshadows the 'revelation' of the story's title presented to us in this vision.

Bibliography

O'Connor, F., "Revelation", in *The Secret Self, Volume 1*, Dent, London, 1985

Comment

The most important thing about this essay is the way it tackles the question - and the way it **doesn't** do it. It begins with a **brief** summary of the plot, but a summary that is clearly intended only to put the passage to be dealt with in its narrative context. There is no other reason for "telling the story" and it is done very briefly.

Then the essay focuses on what the author is "saying" by means of the characters and incidents she has chosen to include, the way she portrays these characters and the viewpoint from which the story is narrated. The writer of the essay has **not** gone through the passage chronologically, picking out relevant details as he came to them -or rather, that isn't what he did in the finished essay.He may well have done that as a step in the analytical process but there is no sign of this in the final version.

The first thing to do with a question like this is to look at the whole story because you can't usefully look at an isolated passage without considering its context. However, you need to look at more than just the events and the characters. You need to consider what the author is "saying" in the story. This may well be completely unexplicit. (The author may not even have been consciously aware of it at the time of writing!) It may only be implied in the way in which the story is told. This is why the "narrative method" is so important. If a story is well written an author's narrative style and language will in some way be organically linked to the story's underlying ideas.Therefore, before you start writing or judging the narrative style of a particular passage you must know what the story is **about** at a deeper level than just story-line. When you are doing this it helps if you keep in your mind the fact that any author has complete control over his or her story. Nothing is given. Anything can be included or omitted. It is therefore fair to assume that everything has been put in for a purpose - conscious or unconscious - and what that purpose is can be understood by looking at the "evidence" - the way the story is told. The act of literary criticism is partly an act of interpretation and, in the case of short stories,this has to begin with an interpretation of the "meaning" or "meanings". Very often this has to be worked at. It will not leap out at you as soon as you read it. You may well not "see" it until you've studied the details and thought about them for some time. The kind of things it may be fruitful to look at are

- why the author chose this particular title

- why the story begins and ends in the way it does

- what the significance of particular incidents is

- who the narrator is and why that particular viewpoint has been chosen

- why particular characters - however minor - have been included

- what you know about each character and why you have been given so much information - or so little.

- whose thoughts are you privy to, and why did the author give you this kind of insight into this person and not others

- whether there is a pattern discernible in the group of characters chosen how the reader is supposed to react to them, and how the author has ensured that this will be your reaction

When you come to write the essay you may well not start with all this. The writer of this essay doesn't. He leaves the explanation of what the story is "about" till the end where it appears to be the natural conclusion to all the analysis that has preceded it. But he didn't actually think of it at this point. He couldn't start writing the essay until he had worked it out. If he had done so the essay would have been just a series of random comments without any focus.

When you know what the story is about and how the meaning is conveyed you can then consider how the passage you were given fits into all this. You will obviously go through it chronologically first. But this should not be the way you actually write about it. You need to look at what emerges from your initial investigations and identify what significant features emerge. But you also need to see if these features fall into any kind of pattern, and what overall impressions emerge. Then you need to identify how this passage relates to the whole. When you come to write the essay you will have organised your observations into sections and you can use references to the text to illustrate the general points you are making. You also need to remember to relate what you are saying about this passage to your interpretation of the whole story at frequent intervals.

This essay has done all of these things and is therefore a good example for you to follow. However, it has been written by someone with an interest in words for their own sake and the ability to use them accurately, however unusual they may be. It is not necessary for you to do this. In fact, unless you are very skilled in using such words it is a good idea to avoid them. Using a vocabulary that you are not totally in control of is a recipe for disaster. It will obscure your meaning rather than help you communicate it.

SECTION 8

ASSESSMENT OF ESSAYS

Assessment criteria

When marking essays tutors will be looking for certain things. The content of essays on different topics will obviously vary but the qualities of an excellent essay will be the same, whatever the subject.

Each department has its own assessment criteria. They should tell you what they are before you write your first essays or reports. The following are fairly typical.

An excellent essay will have the following characteristics

Quality of argument

- The treatment of the subject will reveal a grasp of the underlying principles, issues and concepts as well as more superficial ideas.

- The essay will show an ability to relate ideas and theories to reality and experience.

- It will show an ability to analyse the subject objectively and from a number of different and appropriate perspectives.

- It will have a clear and relevant line of argument consisting of a sequence of ideas, linked logically and explained clearly. This line of argument should deal with all parts of the question.

- It will use appropriate evidence to justify this line of argument and demonstrate an awareness of how the evidence justifies the ideas.

- The approach to the question will include description, explanation and evaluation.

Structure

The essay will have an introduction which includes

- a suitable interpretation of the question,
- an explanation of the key words (where necessary)
- an indication of the line of argument to be followed.

It will have a clear, well controlled and balanced structure that is focused on the main issues.

All parts of the question should be covered, without unnecessary repetition.

Use of source material

A range of **appropriate** sources should have been used - not necessarily books.

There should be evidence that this source material has been
- carefully selected

and ● assimilated into the writer's own argument.

Evidence extracted from source material should be clearly related to points in the argument of this essay and its relevance justified.

The evidence should be appraised critically.

Technical skills

The technicalities of written communication should be accurately and sensibly used. The following are particularly important in this respect:
- paragraphing
- sentence structure
- spelling
- grammar
- punctuation.

Presentation

- The assignment should be presented in the correct format.

- It should be written in an appropriate style.

- Identifying the sources of information, ideas and statistics should be done meticulously.

- There should be an adequate Bibliography.

- It should all be legible! If it is word-processed it should be done accurately but without undue showiness that draws attention to itself and distracts attention from the argument.

 Of the above elements the quality of the argument and the coherence of its structure are by far the most important. If the technicalities are so inaccurate as to make understanding the argument difficult then this will seriously affect the mark. Inability to use evidence convincingly will damage the line of argument and will therefore penalise itself.

Grading criteria: An example

The grading of essays is not such a mystery as it often seems. Some general grading criteria are as follows.

A grade essays   will demonstrate most of these characteristics. An A+ essay will be exceptionally good.

B grade essays   will have a clear and logical argument which is relevant to the question and well constructed. It may well, however, be occasionally flawed in any of these respects. The quality of the argument will be at all times adequate and, possibly, occasionally good. The evaluative element may well be dealt with in inadequate depth and detail. The essay will demonstrate the use of an adequate range of sources and there should be some evidence of appraisal. Presentation and technicalities will be unexceptionable.

C grade essays   may demonstrate some irrelevance and a tendency to rely on description and explanation rather than evaluation. The description and explanation should, however, be well done. There may be signs of lack of objectivity. It may well be loosely structured with some consequent loss of coherence in places. There may be significant lapses in style and the use of the technicalities of written communication but these will not be bad enough to impede communication.

D grade essays	may well lack relevance and structure. It will deal with the topic in a narrow and limited way, using only a narrow range of evidence. There will be some signs of an argument but it may often be weak, unclear, illogical, personalised and unrelated to the evidence. Understanding will be of a very superficial kind and evidence for ideas will be seriously lacking. If significant amounts of source material have been used in an uncritical way, a D will be mandatory.
E grade essays	will be largely irrelevant, unstructured, and show no signs of attempting to argue a case. It will show little evidence of understanding. It may well also suffer from serious inaccuracies in style and the technicalities. Where significant amounts of source material have been used without acknowledgement an E will be mandatory and the student's attention will be drawn to the fact that this is unacceptable practice.

A practical example

Question

Compare and contrast the effects that blindness and deafness have on language development and discuss the adequacy of current theories of language development in the light of your findings.

Answers

Excellent:	1)	Identifies the consequences of blindness and deafness for language development. Groups **Consequences** into significant categories.

	2)	Draws on a wide range of theories from different writers
	3)	Compares and contrasts the theories, drawing conclusions about the nature of language development and relating them to the facts identified in 1).

Good:

1) Identifies the consequences of blindness and deafness for language development.

2) Compares and contrasts some current theories of language development.

3) Identifies the theory/ies that best suit the facts.

Satisfactory:

1) Lists some of the features of blindness and deafness in a reasonable order.

2) Lists some consequences for development including a few for language development.

3) Mentions one or two theories relating to impaired language development

Poor:

1) Writes down everything and anything about blindness, deafness, child development and language development.

2) No justified conclusions drawn and no texts referred to.

3) No obvious order